Volk's Electric Railway

A Visitor's Guide

Brighton & Hove
City Council

Volk's Electric Railway – A Visitor's Guide

First published by Shrewdale Publishing 2018

© Text: Unique Publishing Services Ltd 2018
© Photographs: As credited

Text compiled by Peter Waller

A CIP record for this book is available from the British Library

Shrewdale Publishing is an imprint of Unique Publishing Services Ltd, 3 Merton Court, The Strand, Brighton Marina Village, Brighton BN2 5XY.

www.uniquepublishingservices.com

Printed and bound in Malta by Gutenberg Press Ltd.

ISBN: 978 0 9575898 5 8

Photo credits:
Bill Lucas: 6, 7 (lower), 8 (upper), 8 (lower), 9 (both), 18/19, 57, 58 (both)
John Fox Photography: Front cover (lower), 5, 7 (upper), 8 (middle), 36, 37, 45, 46 (upper), 48, 50, 51, 52, 53, 55 (both), 56 (both), 59 (all), 60 (both), 61 (both), 62 (both), 63 (both), 64
Royal Pavilion & Museums, Brighton & Hove: 10, 11, 12, 13, 14/15, 15 (upper), 16/17, 17 (right), 19 (upper), 20, 21, 23, 29 (lower), 31, 38, 40. 41, 42, 43 (all)
Barry Cross Collection/Online Transport Archive: 22. 24/25, 26/27, 28, 29 (upper), 30, 33, 34, 39, 44, 47 (upper)
John Meredith/Online Transport Archive: Front cover (upper), 32, 46 (lower), 47 (lower), 49
Peter Waller: 35

CONTENTS

FOREWORD

Like so many people, my memories of Volk's Railway stretch back to my childhood. I can recall so clearly riding along Brighton seafront many decades ago, watching intently how the drivers handled the remarkable old electric trains, studying the track layout, marvelling at the depot straddling the tracks close to Halfway station – and generally enjoying the trip.

In 2008, I was asked to declare that summer operating season open. I said I would, as long as I could be shown all aspects of what is a remarkable line. That was gladly granted. Then came the offer I could not resist. Would I like to be trained to drive myself sometimes? There was only one answer: a delighted Yes.

In the years that have followed, I have become greatly involved with this wonderful Victorian engineering gem. It has been a terrific pleasure to enthuse others, especially to encourage the small army of volunteers in the last year or two who have done so much to assist the full-time staff as Magnus Volk's pioneering invention got its 21st century makeover.

Do enjoy this highly informative booklet. Ride on the Volk's, and tell everyone you know about it. And it is quite possible, the driver of your train might be me!

Nicholas Owen

Opposite: Broadcaster and presenter Nicholas Owen seen at the controls of newly-restored No 4.

INTRODUCTION

Welcome to the newly restored Volk's Electric Railway. We hope that you will enjoy your journey along the World's oldest surviving electric railway. During the course of your trip you will see some of Brighton's most important seaside sights. Look out for them as the car makes its way along the seashore.

Palace Pier

Located immediately to the west of Aquarium Station, the enormously popular Palace Pier dates from 1899. It is 525m in length and contains 137km of planking. Repainting the structure takes three months. A star of film, it appeared in such classics as *Brighton Rock* and *Carry on at Your Convenience.*

Palace Pier

Aquarium Station

The western terminus of Volk's Electric Railway was moved to its current location in 1930 when Madeira Drive was widened. The new Visitor Centre & Station – with its interpretative displays covering the history of Magnus Volk and the electric railway – was constructed during 2017 to replace the old station demolished at the end of 2016. The old station was a tram shelter dating from 1901 and placed here in 1948 when the railway reopened after the War.

Madeira Drive

Running parallel to the electric railway is Madeira Drive. This was built on reclaimed land in order to prevent the erosion of the cliffs. It regularly plays host to a wide range of events, such as the annual Veteran Car Run. One feature of the Victorian work is the cast-iron mezzanine terrace that stretches for more than 850m along the road. Known as Madeira Terrace, this offers unparalleled views of events on the road below.

Halfway Station

When the electric railway first opened, it terminated at Paston Place. It was only extended further to the east after Volk's other great railway – the Brighton & Rottingdean Seashore Electric Railway – was closed in 1901. A small ticket office can be seen immediately to the west of the Halfway platforms.

Workshop

With the line extended, a new workshop was constructed at Halfway through which the running line passes. The building seen today is the result of the recent Heritage Lottery Funded project, completed in early 2018.

Banjo Groyne

The Banjo Groyne, so called because of its shape, dates from 1877 and was designed to regulate the coastal currents. Constructed in flint and paving stones, its current form was the result of work undertaken by Magnus Volk in 1884 when it provided the terminus for his electric railway and later for the seashore railway. The line east of the Banjo Groyne was originally built on a viaduct; however, the build up of shingle resulted in the viaduct being buried and it was replaced with normal track.

Duke's Mound

Providing a link between Madeira Drive and Marine Parade, Duke's Mound heads inland immediately to the east of the Banjo Groyne. At the junction is sited No 285 Madeira Drive; these premises were Volk's workshop, and remain in use by the railway today. It was here that, until his death in 1937, Magnus Volk oversaw the management of his most enduring creation.

Duke's Mound

Black Rock Station

Black Rock Station

The eastern terminus of the electric railway is Black Rock. Originally the line extended further to the east, but was cut-back in 1937 when a lido – now demolished – was constructed. The current station dates to the late 1990s and belongs to Southern Water. This was not part of the recent redevelopment work.

THE MAN AND HIS VISION

In an era when innovative and pioneering engineers abounded – think Isambard Kingdom Brunel – there were few more visionary than Magnus Volk.

Volk was born on 19 October 1851 in Brighton at 35 (now 40) Western Road. He was the son of a German-born clockmaker but he was destined to make his mark in a different way – with electricity.

From an early age he demonstrated a talent for experimentation. He built models of equipment like windmills from the parts of old clocks, earning himself the nickname 'Magnus the Dreamer' for his inventiveness.

However, harsh reality was soon to arrive when, at the age of 17, his father died and he took over the family clockmaking business. He demonstrated as much skill in business as he had in his juvenile model-making and the business prospered. It became a major employer, with some 20 members of staff, as Volk expanded its range of products to include parlour telegraph instruments and then electric bells and coils. It was this work that helped foster his new interest in electricity and its potential uses.

On 8 April 1879 Magnus married Anna Banfield of Burgess Hill. In all there were seven children, one of whom, Conrad, wrote a biography of his father. Although the family lived in Brighton for much of the time, between 1889 and 1892, whilst he was running electric launches on the River Thames, they resided in Clapham, then Halliford and Wandsworth. Between 1903 and 1914 Volk lived in Hassocks before once again returning to Brighton and 38 (now 128) Dyke Road, where his residency is remembered with a plaque.

Away from the business, Volk had continued to experiment. In 1879 he built an organ and then linked his house – 40 Preston Road – with that in Springfield Road of a friend, William Jago, using an early telephone. The following year he completed the installation of electric lighting in his house. More significantly he displayed 'Swan's Incandescent Electric Lamps' at the Brighton Health Congress and Domestic & Scientific Exhibition held in December 1881 in the Royal Pavilion.

In 1881 he relocated his business to larger premises at 25 Ditchling Rise; here he demonstrated the installation of a fire alarm that was linked directly to the local police

> **The Southern Railway regarded Magnus Volk as 'the Father of electric traction' and bestowed many honours on him.**

Above: Magnus Volk (1851–1937).

station. The alarm system was adopted for the Brighton Health Congress, held later that year and Volk was awarded a gold medal.

Volk was not the only pioneer of electricity in Brighton; a 'competitor' to him was Robert Hammond, who had demonstrated arc lighting to representatives of the Corporation in 1881. Despite this, the Corporation employed Volk to light the Royal Pavilion for a concert in 1882. The following year he was invited back to light the whole building.

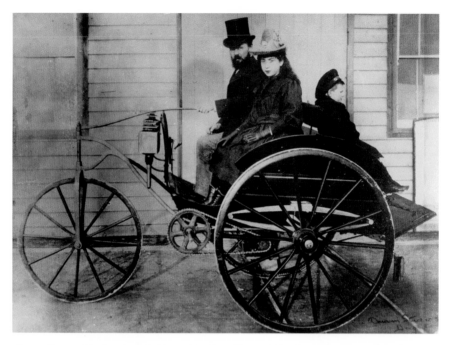

Above: Pictured in October 1887 outside the offices of his electric railway on Madeira Drive, Magnus Volk is at the controls of his pioneering electric dog-cart.

Whilst this work was in hand, he had begun the project for which he is perhaps best remembered: Volk's Electric Railway. He had seen a small demonstration railway built by Siemens at Crystal Palace in 1881, which excited him and he was determined to build his own. Magnus had previously been asked to supply an electric motor to a London company but the customer had cancelled the order. Experimenting with the motor, a Siemens-built dynamo and a 2hp gas engine, Magnus had enough equipment to power an electric railway. Approaching the Corporation, for whom he had become Electrical Engineer, he was granted permission to construct a short experimental 2ft 0in gauge line along the seafront. The gas engine and dynamo were installed in a makeshift power station and the energy, generated at 50V, was transmitted to the single electric carriage to power it through the small motor. The line took 18 days to

In 1917 Magnus designed an egg-cup for a one-armed ex-serviceman.

Above: Pictured around 1910 Magnus Volk can be seen seated in a petrol-powered car; earlier in his career he had pioneered the development of electric cars – indeed one that he produced was sold to the Sultan of the Ottoman Empire.

construct, running from the Aquarium to the Chain Pier.

With the Mayor of Brighton at its controls, the line opened on 4 August 1883 and proved immensely popular with subsequent extensions being made. The early years were ones of considerable struggle. To quote from Volk's obituary published in the *Meccano Magazine* of 1937: 'Mr Volk fought pluckily against misfortunes of all kinds, however, and he received so much support locally that he was able to keep his line open and to retain complete control of it.'

However, this did not stop Volk falling into financial difficulties. In 1887 Volk constructed a prototype electric car that he demonstrated on the Parade in Brighton. This led to an order from the Sultan of Turkey, Abdul Hamid, for a car (as well as an electric launch two years later). The Sultan's car was built by the Brighton-based carriage builders of Pack & Sons with a motor supplied by Moritz Immisch of London. Volk himself took it to Istanbul in order to demonstrate its capabilities, but no further cars were ordered. By now Volk was in financial difficulties and, in January 1888, he filed for bankruptcy. It was not until August 1891 that he was discharged and, in October the same year, it was announced that; 'Mr Magnus Volk has entered into possession of the Electric Railway at Brighton.'

With the railway secured, Volk's ambition turned to an extension eastwards to reach Rottingdean. Volk's determination was demonstrated by the end result – the Brighton & Rottingdean Seashore Electric Railway – which was undoubtedly one of the strangest, if paradoxically practical, railways ever constructed in the British Isles. A single electric boat-shaped carriage ran on parallel tracks on the seabed. It was supported above the high water level by four steel stilts and took its power from an overhead wire strung on poles along the route. The carriage was officially named 'Pioneer' but it quickly gained the nickname 'Daddy Longlegs'. The railway opened on 28 November 1896 but just six days later was severely damaged by a great storm during the night of 4/5 December.

Rough Sea at Volk's Electric Railway, Brighton

Above: The sea can be a dangerous neighbour, as Volk discovered on several occasions. Both the electric railway and later the Brighton & Rottingdean were to suffer severely from storm damage during their history.

Below: The Brighton seafront in the period before the First World War. As a car makes its way towards the line's then western terminus, bathing machines can be seen waiting for customers on the beach as a party of ladies make their way along Madeira Drive.

Magnus Volk, though shocked by the damage, resolved to rebuild the railway and it re-opened on 20 July 1897. For the next three years it was a great attraction but coastal erosion led Brighton Corporation to start building more groynes near Black Rock and the railway was forced to close, the last journey being made in January 1901.

Following the closure of the Brighton & Rottingdean Seashore Electric Railway and the

extension of the Volk's Electric Railway to the east, Volk himself spent the next 30 years running the business from his offices at 285 Madeira Drive. His final public appearance was on 7 May 1937 at the formal opening of the new Black Rock Station.

Magnus Volk died on 20 May 1937 at the age of 86. He was buried in the churchyard of St Wulfran's church in Ovingdean, near Brighton.

Above: An early flyer promoting the attractions of Volk's Electric Railway.

Left: With crowds onboard, on the platform and on the Banjo Groyne, Volk's extraordinary Brighton & Rottingdean Seashore Electric Railway was certainly – if only briefly – a major attraction.

Below: The offices of Volk's Electric Railway: Duke's Mound – 285 Madeira Drive, Brighton – still the home of the railway after more than a century.

Right: By the early 1930s the electric railway was managed by Volk and his son Herman. In 1933, to celebrate the line's 50th anniversary, they hosted a private luncheon. This is the invitation issued to another son – Conrad – who was later to write the biography of his father.

Volk's Electric Railway Jubilee
1883-1933

Mr. Magnus Volk & Mr. M. H. Volk
request the pleasure of the company of

Mr Conrad Volk

at a small private Luncheon at the Royal Albion Hotel on Friday, 4th August, 1933, at 1 o'clock.

R.S.V.P. The Secretary,
Volk's Electric Railway,
Brighton.

VOLK'S ELECTRIC RAILWAY,

Memoranda Re Volk's Electric Railway.

BRIGHTON   December 27th./30.

TELEGRAMS:
ELECTRIC RAILWAY, BRIGHTON.
TELEPHONE:
BRIGHTON 1578.

A Siemen's D.5. (? 6.5.) was first used to light my house
which led to my appointment as Electrical Engineer to The
Corporation with Incandescent Lamps (Carbon Type) this
Mr. Alexander Siemens told me was at that time one of the largest
installations then existing.

This small Dynamo was used as aGenerator for the
original Electric Railway which ran during that Summer; in
April 1884 the larger extended line was opened the Generator being
a Siemens D.2. (about 7.5. H.P.) the Motors being flat,series
wound , with rocking brushes for reversing , later on a larger
Siemens Generator was used, these were eventually placed in cars
as motors, and with the flat Motors have been at work continu-
-ously driving the Cars up till the present time and can be
seen at work daily. The Original D.5. is in the possession of
The Technical School here though how they obtained possession
of it I cannot remember.

Magnus Volk

Above: On 27 December 1930 Volk penned a memorandum outlining the history of
the line. It concludes: 'The original D.5 [dynamo] is in the possession of the Technical
School here though how they obtained possession of it I cannot remember.'

VOLK'S ELECTRIC RAILWAY

To misquote an advert, the future's bright, the future's ... electricity. During the second half of the 19th century, scientists and inventors across much of the globe had been looking at electricity, its properties and what it was possible to achieve with it. In 1880 the first electric tram was demonstrated by Fyodor Pirotsky in St Petersburg. He converted a horse tram for the purpose. The following year Werner von Siemens introduced an electrified service to the Lichterfelde district of Berlin whilst also

Above: The opening of the line on 4 August 1883 with the clock tower at the Aquarium in the background. On the right-hand platform is the Mayor of Brighton whilst on the left-hand one is Magnus Volk.

Above: A view of the original terminus at Palace Pier in 1904 when an official French visit was made to Brighton in celebration of the Entente Cordiale signed by Britain and France that year. The poster advertises ' Running along beach at places over the sea for a return fare of 4d (2p).

operating a demonstration line outside the Crystal Palace in London.

Volk was a customer of Siemens – he had acquired a Siemens-built dynamo to light his home in 1880 – and would have been aware of these developments. Thus when the London customer defaulted on the order for an electric motor, Volk wrote to the town clerk on 14 June 1883 to seek permission to construct a 2ft 0in gauge line along the seafront at Brighton.

Although there were objections, permission was given surprisingly quickly; so fast, in fact, that it was possible to open the line on 4 August 1883 with the mayor, Arthur Cox, at the controls of a small electric carriage (or car). The new line, which extended for about quarter-of-a-mile, was lightly laid on the shingle beach. The gas engine and dynamo required to power the car were housed in an arch under the promenade belonging to the Royal Humane Society. The power supply fed the two running rails – akin to a model railway – with the track laid on wooden sleepers. Its top speed was 6mph.

The popularity of the line was immediate but, in September 1883, it faced its first assault by the sea leading to some damage. Buoyed by the success of the railway, Volk approached the Corporation with plans to extend westwards to the boundary with Hove. This was rejected so he sought to go east and the Corporation granted him a lease as far as Paston Place.

For the line's reopening and extension, Volk adopted a wider gauge – 2ft 8½in – that is still in use today, although he retained the principle of the power being transmitted by the two running rails. The new line operated at 160 volts. One feature of the extension was the timber-lined cutting that permitted the cars to pass through the shingle and under the Chain Pier.

During the busy months, Magnus would stand on the balcony at Paston Place with a pair of powerful binoculars watching the progress of the cars.

Below: Brighton's famous Chain Pier; opened in 1823, this 1,134ft-long structure was to survive until destroyed in the same storm in December 1896 that seriously damaged the Electric Railway. In order to pass under the pier, Volk constructed a short cutting for the electric railway that was timber lined.

THE OLD CHAIN PIER, BRIGHTON.
BUILT 1823. DESTROYED DEC. 4TH 1896.

COPYRIG
857 WARDEL

Following completion of Palace Pier in 1901, the Electric Railway's station was rebuilt and renamed after the pier.

PALACE PIER, BRIGHTON.

Above: An early view of the Volk's Electric Railway station at Paston Place and its associated depot. Until 1901 passengers could change here onto the sea-going railway. Stretching into the sea is the Banjo Groyne; now Grade II listed, this structure dates from 1877 but its current form owes much to the arrival of the railway in 1884.

The rebuilt and extended line opened with due ceremony on 4 April 1884 although not without incident: the inaugural car derailed, probably as a result of being overloaded. December 1884 saw the line once again afflicted by storm damage – this was to be a regular hazard for the line with repeat occurrences in 1886, 1891, 1896, 1903, 1929 and 1931 – but the damage was always repaired. One modification – made during 1886 – was

to install a third (power-carrying) rail. This was designed to reduce current leakages caused by the presence of sea water.

The line prospered through the remainder of the century although towards the end of the period, Volk's attention was diverted to the development of the line to Rottingdean. It was the demise of this line that led to the next significant development to the electric railway. In order to replace the Rottingdean service beyond Paston Place, Volk proposed an extension of the existing line to Black Rock. This was approved by the Corporation in February 1901 and opened three months later; the extension took the length of the line from 1,400 yards to 1¼ miles. The extension eastwards was built upon a short viaduct immediately adjacent

Volk's Electric Railway, Brighton.   A.E.B 1507

Above: When the eastern extension of the electric railway first opened in mid- 1901, the line was carried on a viaduct above the shingle and sea. This undated view – but probably photographed in the 1920s – is also notable for the wonderful motor charabancs and coaches parked in the background.

to Paston Place. The influence of the new groynes – one of the factors in the demise of the Rottingdean line – resulted in the build-up of shingle, with the result that the viaduct was eventually buried.

Also in 1901 a new company – Magnus Volk Ltd – was registered and the assets of the railway were vested in this new company. A further boost to the line's revenues came in 1903 when Volk was permitted to operate on Sundays. In 1911 the original, rather basic, terminus at Black Rock was replaced by a new structure, affectionately known as 'The Bungalow'. The new station, which retained the two platforms of the original, was a single-storey chalet like structure that offered a considerably enhanced presence over the old small hut.

In 1923, following financial reconstruction, ownership passed to a new

Above: The Bungalow station at Black Rock; the development of the lido meant that the line was cut back and a new station constructed.

Below: Happy passengers enjoy the line during the 1930s; the next decade would see considerable changes to the railway as Brighton Corporation took over.

Above: It's the summer of 1939 and although war clouds were in the air, few would have imagined that it would be almost a decade before the line would operate again and by that stage would be under new ownership.

Magnus Volk Ltd but, as the 1920s wore on, the line was under threat. In 1928 the Corporation was keen to widen Maderia Road (later Drive) and construct a new bathing pool close to the Aquarium. The threat was, however, averted. The road was widened but the bathing pool was not constructed, Volk was asked to foreshorten the line at its western end by 200 yards. By way of compensation he was given permission to build a much larger and grander station at the new Aquarium terminus and this was opened on 27 June 1930.

On 4 August 1933 the line celebrated its 50th anniversary. As at the line's opening in 1883, the event was graced by the presence of the current Mayor, Frank Beal, who travelled the route in the company of the line's 81-year-old founder.

Above: With Palace Pier and the terminus of the Volk's Electric Railway in the background, Brighton beach is prepared for a possible invasion with barbed wire, tank traps and concrete blocks as the country's first line of defence.

Although earlier proposals to construct a bathing pool at the western end had been abandoned, the Corporation decided to build a lido at Black Rock. This opened in 1937 and resulted in a further reduction in the line's length by another 200 yards. The line now extended for just over a mile. A new station at Black Rock, capable of dealing with the crowds attracted by the new lido opened on 7 May 1937. Less than a fortnight later, the line's founder was to die. Herman Volk, one of Volk's sons, took over the control of the railway. However, there was soon to be a much more significant change.

Throughout its history the line had operated on a series of leases from the Corporation; these, however, could easily not be renewed. Under the Brighton Corporation (Transport) Act of 1938 the Corporation was given the powers to operate the railway and, on 1 April 1940, it formally took over

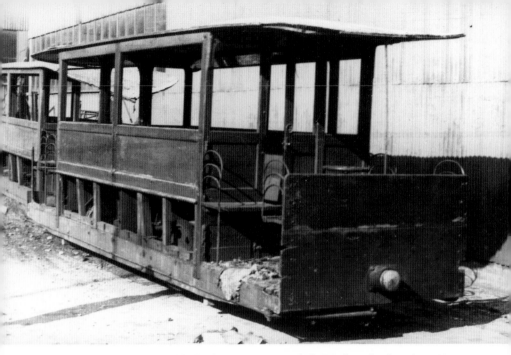

Above: Wartime storage and lack of maintenance took their toll on the fleet; here Nos 1 and 2 of 1884 and 1885 await their fate at Lewes Road depot in May 1948.

ownership and operation of the line. It was an alarming time for the new owners to take possession. With the threat of an imminent German invasion, the government closed all the beaches and operation of the railway was suspended on 2 July 1940. Although the line and sheds at Paston Place were left intact, the stations at Aquarium and Black Rock were demolished as the beach was prepared as part of the front-line against a possible Nazi invasion. Services would not operate again until peace returned and the line was restored.

The wartime years led to a considerable deterioration in the rolling stock with three cars beyond repair and the line itself, over and above the demolitions undertaken in 1940, in a poor condition. Brighton Corporation was faced with two options: to abandon the railway completely or try to re-open it with as little cost as possible. Thankfully they chose the latter. Before services could be reintroduced, the track was relaid, a new terminus was constructed at Black Rock, the depot at Paston Place was reconstructed, a new structure – a redundant tramway shelter – was installed at the Aquarium terminus, second-hand cars were acquired from Southend Pier and the bulk of the fleet was refurbished at the Corporation's Lewes Road depot.

With the repair work completed, services were reintroduced on 15 May 1948. At this time the line operated throughout the year; however, services were suspended during the winter of 1952/53. This was to permit a further overhaul and, from the end of 1954, services have generally operated for the summer season only with occasional winter use over the festive season.

For much of the line's history, the cars appeared in a varnished wood livery; in the early 1960s this was replaced by a livery of dark brown and yellow with the letters 'V' and 'R' being carried on the front and rear of each vehicle. This change occurred after control of the line passed from the Corporation's Transport Department to the Entertainments & Publicity Committee. Increasingly the line was perceived as a leisure facility rather than as a

> In the early days of the Motor Speed Trials, Magnus Volk would put seats on the top of the sheds and charge 1/- (5p) for a grandstand view! Spectators could also enjoy tea and cakes.

Below: In 1964 there was a significant change in operation when the cars started to operate as coupled trains. Here, in September 1970, Nos 1 and 2 are seen together heading towards Aquarium.

means of public transport.

The 1960s saw the railway still carrying more than half-a-million passengers annually although economies (such as the alteration to the trackwork at the two termini) were undertaken to keep the line viable. Sadly from the start of the following decade the finances started to decline. The growth in the overseas package holiday had resulted in a decline in those opting to have a traditional British seaside holiday and, in 1978, the closure of the lido at Black Rock led to a further decline in patronage.

There was a serious risk, given that the railway was now loss-making and in an increasingly parlous condition, that the line might disappear. With the development of the Marina, approved in 1975 with work starting later that year, consideration was given to the railway's replacement with something capable of handling the traffic that the Marina was expected to generate. The line celebrated its centenary on 4 August 1983 – in the

Below: In 1983 the railway celebrated its centenary; to mark the anniversary Nos 3 and 4 were suitably decorated. They're seen here on 6 August 1983 two days after the centenary special was driven by Volk's then only surviving son, the 83-year-old Conrad.

presence of Conrad Volk, Volk's only surviving son – but was considered by many to be living on borrowed time.

However, despite the threat to its future, the line survived although it did face two physical challenges. The first of these was human: in May 1987 an arson attack saw one car almost destroyed and two others damaged. The other was physical. By the early 1990s, the viaduct erected in 1901 on the extension from Paston Place eastwards but subsequently buried by shingle had reached the end of its life. During 1991, the viaduct was replaced by a concrete raft. This required the temporary closure of the section from Paston Place from the end of the 1990 season; it finally reopened on 26 September 1991. Later in the decade the line was

> There was a model of the Royal Sussex County Hospital in the Booking Office at Black Rock station with a donation box next to it.

Below: In September 1993 the existing Black Rock station – called at the time Marina – was coming to the end of its life; evidence is in hand that construction was shortly to get underway on the current structure. For a period the line was known as 'Volk's Excursion Railway'.

temporarily shortened by 70 yards to permit the construction of a storm water storage scheme for the Marina. This resulted in the construction of a new single-platform station at Black Rock, which opened in 1998. The building belongs to Southern Water and accommodates a pumping station.

In the last decade of the 20th and first decade of the 21st century, the country's oldest surviving electric railway seemed to be doing just that – surviving. A volunteer group – the Volk's Electric Railway Association (VERA) – was established in 1995 to support the line and its operation but there was a widespread impression that the future was not rosy.

All that, however, was to change with the announcement in 2015 that the Heritage Lottery Fund had made a grant of £1.65 million to see the line refurbished and its rolling stock repaired. The project was also backed by VERA. Truly a new era for this fascinating piece of Britain's history beckoned.

Above: The old order at Halfway: the interior of the old depot with the line's diesel shunter on the left. The poor condition of this building was one reason for the restoration project.

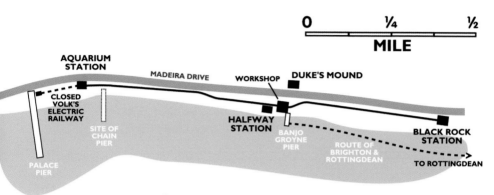

0   ¼   ½

MILE

AQUARIUM STATION

MADEIRA DRIVE

WORKSHOP

DUKE'S MOUND

CLOSED VOLK'S ELECTRIC RAILWAY

SITE OF CHAIN PIER

HALFWAY STATION

BANJO GROYNE PIER

ROUTE OF BRIGHTON & ROTTINGDEAN

BLACK ROCK STATION

TO ROTTINGDEAN

PALACE PIER

VOLK'S ELECTRIC RAILWAY

Above: The end of an era: a final view of the old Aquarium station at the end of the 2016 season before demolition work commenced.

PIONEER AT SEA

Volk was nothing if not ambitious. Having established his electric railway and extended it to Paston Place, he was determined to see the service extend eastwards to Rottingdean. However, the unfavourable lie of the land meant that Volk had to come up with a radical solution. The end result was one of the most extraordinary and innovative railways ever constructed in Britain.

In 1893 a new company – the Brighton & Rottingdean Seashore Electric Railway – was incorporated by Volk. With Richard St George Moore appointed engineer, work started on the line's construction in 1894. With the cost of a viaduct at the Paston Place end being deemed too expensive, Volk decided to construct his line partly through the sea. At its maximum

Above: A view records the Brighton & Rottingdean car arriving at Paston Place; the picture shows to good effect the lifeboat that had to be carried.

distance the track was about 100m from the shore with the rails laid on concrete sleepers embedded in the seabed.

The track as laid consisted of two parallel sets of rails, each set 825mm apart; the notional overall gauge of the line – from outer rail to outer rail – was 5.5m. The line was supplied with a single car built by the Gloucester Railways Carriage & Wagon Co. The car looked almost boat-like, constructed on four legs each of which were 7m in length and was officially called *Pioneer*; unofficially, however, it was nicknamed *Daddy Long-Legs*.

The remains of the steel gantry over the sea from the eastern side of Banjo Groyne can still be seen on the north side of the track.

Inevitably, such a quirky vehicle was to cause some confusion as to its operation. Following discussion, the car was designated as a sea- going vessel. This meant that it was the only railway in Britain that had to be

Above: Designated as a sea-going vessel, the Brighton & Rottingdean car was also fitted with lifebelts and was controlled by a driver who also had to be a qualified captain of a sea-going vessel.

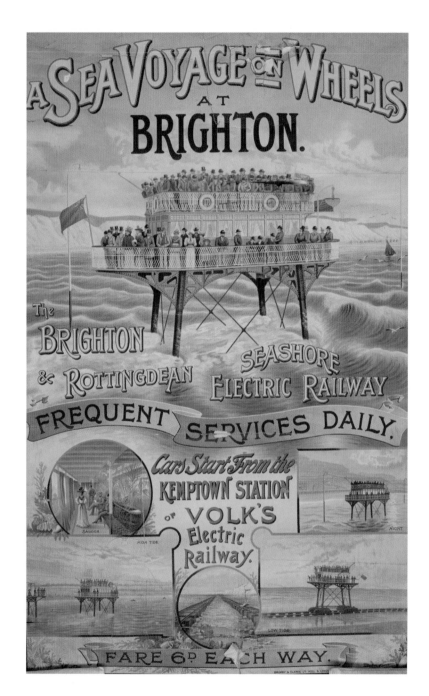

Above: A view from the beach; the scale of the line must have been impressive to those looking up at it.

Left: The Brighton & Rottingdean was promoted as 'A sea voyage on wheels'. Flying the red ensign, *Pioneer* is very much a vessel at sea.

Above: The Brighton & Rottingdean car stood on four 7m-long legs; each of these was fitted with a small four-wheel truck that ran on a pair of rails set 825mm apart. These pairs of rails were set on concrete sleepers with the outer rail of each pair being set 5½m apart.

staffed by a driver who also had to be a qualified captain of a sea-going vessel and be fitted with lifebelts and a lifeboat. As a result, the line was promoted as 'A sea voyage on wheels'.

It took two years for the three-mile line to be completed before being opened on 28 November 1896 but it was not to last long. On 4 December 1896, a severe storm caused serious damage to the line with *Pioneer* being knocked on its side.

Volk, however, was not discouraged; the line was restored and the car repaired – with its height slightly raised – with services being reintroduced on 20 July 1897. The line was popular – carrying some 45,000 in its first year – but suffered from being slow (particularly at high tide) and Volk could not afford to install improved motors.

Lack of power was not the only problem that afflicted the line; in 1900 services were suspended for two months when it was discovered that recently erected groynes had caused underwater scouring of the concrete sleepers. Shortly after, the Corporation decided to construct a beach protection barrier; this required Volk to divert the line. Without the funds so to do, he closed the line in January 1901.

Following closure, the line was dismantled with the track and car sold for scrap. At low water, it is still possible to see the sleepers in the seabed whilst Volk's model of the prototype car is on display in the Volk's Electric Railway Visitor Centre.

Above: The interior of the passenger compartment on *Pioneer*; this measured 12ft 6in by 25ft 3in and was luxuriously appointed with comfortable seating and potted plants. It also had electric lighting.

Left: After the storm of 1896 *Pioneer* was rebuilt; the most obvious difference was the reconstruction of the central support struts below the floor of the vehicle.

Right: A flyer promoting the Brighton & Rottingdean Electric Railway; given the line's location, the caveat 'Weather and circumstances permitting' was probably prudent.

THE FLEET

Over the years the Volk's Electric Railway has operated a variety of cars with a number either being scrapped or are no longer based on the line.

When the line was first opened in 1883, it was operated by a single 10-seat car – No 1 – built by William Pollard. Little is known about this particular vehicle other than it was impractical to regauge when the line was modified from 2ft to 2ft 8½in and was scrapped in 1884.

Following the rebuilding of the line, two new 30-seat cars were acquired; one – a new No 1 (renumbered 5 in 1897 and reverting to No 1 in 1928) – was delivered in 1884 and the second – No 2 – the following year. These two cars could accommodate 30 passengers – six on each of the open platforms and 18 in an enclosed central saloon. When new the saloons had embossed plate-glass windows with blue silk curtains and ceilings with hand-painted flowers. These two cars were to survive in service until 1940 (although devoid of the curtains by this date). However, inadequate storage

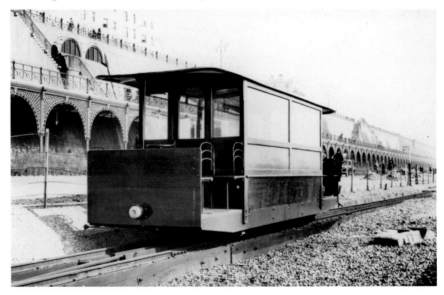

Above: No 2 was built in 1885 and was the second car delivered to the newly regauged railway. Seen here on 6 March 1938, it was to be placed in store during the war but never operated again. The car's livery is varnished wood.

Above: In 1892 the fleet was augmented by two new cars – Nos 3 and 4 – which are, today, the oldest surviving vehicles owned by the railway. The latter is seen at Halfway in 1978. When new, the two were crossbench cars and lacked the closed compartment.

Many of the cars were built in the workshop at Paston Place which for some years was connected to the line by a track and a turntable on the eastern side of the sheds.

during the war took its toll and, after being removed to the corporation's Lewes Road depot in 1947, they were scrapped in June the following year.

The fleet was supplemented in 1892 by the acquisition of two new cars – Nos 3 and 4. These were built by the railway itself at Paston Place and, when built, were fitted with an experimental drive invented by a friend of Volk, Anthony Reckenzaun, and manufactured by the Leeds-based company of Greenwood & Batley Ltd. This equipment resulted in passengers being warned to 'step over shaft' as they were confronted by a wooden bar above the drive shaft impeding their progress. This slightly unsatisfactory arrangement survived until replacement

Above: Three cars were acquired in 1901 for the extension; the first of the trio was No 6; it is seen here approaching the Aquarium terminus in 1978.

Below: Pictured outside the depot on 4 May 1952 is No 5;. built new as No 8 in 1901, it and No 7 were the first cars to be designed with side entrance doors.

Above: In 1930, the railway acquired a fully-enclosed car designed for winter use; this short-lived vehicle is pictured outside the depot in September 1935.

Below: Seen at Black Rock on 4 June 1950 is No 1; this car had originally been No 10 when built in 1926 but had been renumbered in 1948.

Above: In 1910 No 9 was built; between 1948 and 2000 this car was numbered 2 and, in this condition, it is pictured in 1959.

equipment was installed in 1901. In 1923 both cars received rebuilt underframes whilst the bodies of both were also modified. In 1963 No 3, as the car closest to original condition, was decorated to mark the line's 80th anniversary. No 4 has been fully restored by Alan Keef Ltd as part of the recent refurbishment whilst No 3 is being restored by the Volk's Electric Railway Association.

The line's third No 1 was a 30-seat saloon car again built at Paston Place; this adopted the chain-and-belt drive as utilised in the earlier Nos 1 and 2 of 1884/85 and was completed in 1897. This particular car was to be relatively short-lived; it was taken out of service and scrapped in 1928.

Following the extension of the line in 1901, three new cars appeared; Nos 6-8 were again constructed by the railway at Paston Place. Fitted with Belgian-made electric motors, these cars could accommodate 32 passengers originally – 16 in the enclosed central compartment and eight on each of the end open platforms – but each of the trio has been subsequently lengthened, allowing a total of 40 passengers now to be carried. Nos 7 and 8 were the first cars in the fleet to be designed with side entrance doors. Between 1948 and 2000, No 8 was numbered 5. No 6 was the second car restored at Alan Keef Ltd as part of the current restoration project whilst Nos 7 and 8 are operational.

> The overhead controllers on the Volk's cars were changed to dashboard controllers in 1962–63.

The fleet was further increased in 1910 by the construction of No 9; this was again built at Paston Place and was the first car constructed that could accommodate 40 passengers from new. Also fitted with a Belgian-built motor, it was numbered 2 between 1948 and 2000; now again No 9, the car is part of the operational fleet.

The fleet remained nine strong until, in 1926, No 10 was constructed.

Above: In order to replace cars lost as a result of the lack of wartime maintenance, two ex-Southend Pier cars were acquired in 1948; this is the first of the two – No 8 – on 4 June 1950 shortly after it had entered service.

Above: Work in progress on car maintenance at the old depot; concerns about the condition of this structure were one factor in the decision to undertake the line's refurbishment.

This was a further 40-seat vehicle built at Paston Place utilising a Belgian-built motor. Renumbered 1 between 1948 and 2000, No 10 is the third of the cars restored by Alan Keef Ltd.

Following the withdrawal of No 1 in 1927 and the renumbering of No 1 back to No 5, a second No 5 was acquired in 1930. This was built by the Hove-based Kelsey's Motor Works and was powered by a Siemens- built motor. It was a 24-seat fully enclosed vehicle designed for winter operation. Unusually its side-panels were painted – in a royal blue and cream livery – instead of being simply stained and varnished; this was because it was constructed in steel rather than the wood used for the side panels on earlier cars. Wartime storage and lack of maintenance resulted in the vehicle's deterioration after cessation of services in 1940. Like Nos 1 and 2, No 5 was transferred to Lewes Road depot in 1947 and scrapped by the end of the following year.

With the loss of vehicles due to the ravages of war and recognising that the full service required eight cars, in September 1949 two cars were acquired from a Benfleet-based dealer. These were two trailers that had been originally supplied to the pier tramway at Southend-on- Sea and were available at £10 each. The new Nos 8 and 9 were originally built by Falcon Works of Loughborough and, after regauging and remotoring, entered service in Brighton in 1950 and 1953 respectively. Although having a notional capacity of 48 (following rebuilding by Brush – successors to the Falcon Works – in 1911), the seating capacity on Volk's was usually 40. These two cars were withdrawn in the early 1990s. No 8 is now part of Chelmsford Museum's collection and is being restored as a static exhibit and No 9 is at the South Downs Heritage Centre, Hassocks.

Apart from the passenger cars, the line has had – since 1998 – a small diesel engine for use on engineering trains when the power is switched off. This was completed by Alan Keef Ltd in 1988 and originally supplied to Butterley Brick Co Ltd, where it remained until the company's brick works at Star Lane, Rochford in Essex, closed.

Following the completion of the current work, the railway will have seven passenger cars; two of these – Nos 3 and 4 – date originally from 1892, three – Nos 6-8 – from 1901 whilst Nos 9 and 10 date from 1910 and 1926 respectively.

Above: The only non-electric vehicle operated by the railway is a small diesel engine that has been based on the line since 1998; it is seen here during the line's reconstruction in 2017.

THE RESTORATION

After some years where its continued existence was in doubt, Volk's Electric Railway was given a new future in 2015 when it was announced that the Heritage Lottery Fund was prepared to back a project to see the line and its rolling stock restored.

Although both 2013 and 2014 had witnessed reasonable levels of passenger usage – higher than in previous years – the long-term position of the railway was not good. The workshops and depot at Halfway had been condemned and needed urgent replacement. Some of the historic rolling stock was in poor condition and required major restoration. There was also no space to share the important history of Magnus Volk and the railway. These, and a range of other issues, had to be factored into the planned restoration.

With funding in place, work started. A comprehensive report on the line, its future and how it could offer an enhanced visitor attraction was compiled. One of the primary motives was that any development had to be as sustainable as possible. The project's architects were the locally based

Above: A car in kit form: the scene at Alan Keef Ltd in September 2016 with the replacement underframe and roof for one of the three Volk's cars being restored

Above: It's 11 November 2016 and work is well in hand on the demolition of the depot and workshops.

ABIR Architects Ltd; this award-winning company specialises in the design of community-led sustainable buildings. The Yorkshire-based PLB Projects Ltd, a leading design consultancy for museums and galleries, was contracted to undertake the work on the new displays, providing visitors with a comprehensive account of the history of the line and of its creator.

Once the plans had been approved, it was possible for the project to commence. With services having ceased on 4 September 2016 at the end of the summer season, physical work could start in earnest. Late October 2016 witnessed the demolition of Aquarium Station and of the old depot at Banjo Groyne; unfortunately the discovery of an unexpected gas pipe at the latter delayed work. The demolition at the depot was complex, requiring the careful removal of the scaffolding that had supported the roof for 15 years!

The fact that no services could be operated during the summer of 2017 meant that additional track work could be completed. The relaying of the East Loop saw the replacement of the concrete sleepers that had first been laid in 1946 as part of the post-war refurbishment. The additional track work undertaken means that the line is now up to standard to see it into the next decade with only routine maintenance required in future years.

The new station and visitor centre at Aquarium, constructed during the summer of 2017, sees impressive new buildings. As well as providing an exhibition of artefacts and information relating to the history of Magnus Volk and the railway, the new space also acts as a ticket office.

The new workshop was also constructed during 2017; this building will provide secure accommodation for the cars as well as a modern environment for their maintenance. A Visitor Gallery at the workshop is also open to visitors, providing information about the line's operation and how it is maintained. One of the features of the line's operation over the years is that the cars in service pass through the depot en route to Black Rock; in a nice gesture to the line's history, this feature has been retained for the future.

Alongside improvements to the physical structures, work for the project also included the refurbishment of three of the line's historic cars – Nos 4, 6 and 10. These were sent to one of the country's leading specialists in narrow gauge railway equipment – Alan Keef Ltd of Ross-on-Wye in Herefordshire.

The work undertaken on the three cars was substantial, reflecting the fact that two of them are over 100 years old and the third 90. The three cars were moved to the contractors during the autumn of 2016 and work commenced. The work has included the construction of new underframes for all cars. As much as 35–40% of the original structures and fittings have been retained and reinserted on the restored cars. This means that the cars can be considered as having been restored rather than replaced by replicas. Fully restored, the three cars returned to Brighton in time for the 2018 season. Their return means that the line will have six operational passenger cars, with a seventh currently under restoration by the Volk's Electric Railway Association (VERA).

By late 2017 work on the various elements of the restoration project were beginning to come together. One of the restored cars was delivered from Alan Keef Ltd whilst the fitting out of the new Visitor Centre with its displays proceeded. Fitting out of the workshop meant that the cars could be returned to their historic base.

With all now in place, everything was ready for the official relaunch of the line on 13 October 2017. The completion of this project means that one of Britain's best-loved and most historically important attractions is fit for purpose for further generations. Magnus Volk's remarkable innovation – and Britain's and the world's oldest surviving electric railway – can now look forward to its 150th anniversary in 2033.

Above: By March 2017, restoration work on car No 4 is proceeding apace in Ross-on-Wye. Here the wheel sets have been installed into the new underframe and electric motor is about to be refitted.

Below: April 2017 sees progress well in hand on the new workshop at Halfway with the first track laid and the foundations for the structure in place.

Above: With Palace Pier in the background, part of the new Aquarium Station has just been delivered by road on 15 June 2017 and work is in hand to move it across Madeira Drive to its new location.

Below: The new Aquarium Station carefully lifted into place overnight during June 2017.

Above: Construction work continues apace on the new Aquarium Station in August 2017.

Below: With the depot nearing completion in September 2017 the first of the cars are seen again on the railway.

The 1998-built station at Black Rock, which also accommodates a Southern Water pumping station, awaits the return of services in September 2017.

Above: Following the completion of its restoration by Alan Keef Ltd, one of the cars is unloaded at the railway suitably protected for its journey from Herefordshire.

Right: In good traditional railway tradition, the newly-restored cars have builder's plates recognising the contribution of those undertaking the work.

Below: The completed Aquarium Station & Visitor Centre – an attractive facility that enhances the experience that the visitor will have on the world's oldest surviving electric railway.

READY FOR THE NEW ERA

Right: The newly restored Volk's Electric Railway was officially launched on Friday 13 October 2017; guest of honour was Nicholas Owen, who is seen here at the controls of one of the cars on the day.

Above: Following the official opening, services operated between Aquarium and Halfway for the remainder of the 2017 season. No 8 stands in Aquarium station as passengers board during this six-week period.

Above and below: The interior of the new Aquarium station features displays relating to the history of the line as well as the ticket office.

Above: Newly restored No 4 gleams in the autumnal sunshine following the completion of work by Alan Keef Ltd.

Above: Posed on the through running line at the rebuilt depot is No 4; historically the cars have always operated through the depot and the newly refurbished line maintains that tradition. The car returned to use on 22 March 2018 following its restoration.

Above: The new workshop completed – a vast improvement on the life-expired structure that it replaced.

Above: The underside of one of the newly restored cars viewed from the inspection pit in the new workshop. The facilities and workmanship in evidence should ensure that Volk's Electric Railway can look forward to its 150th anniversary with confidence.

Above: It's March 2018 and passengers flock to travel over the newly restored line. With work largely completed, the world's oldest surviving electric railway can look forward with confidence to the next phase in its long and illustrious history.

VOLK'S ELECTRIC RAILWAY ASSOCIATION

The Volk's Electric Railway Association – or VERA as it has become known – was launched upon an unsuspecting public on 16 September 1995. Since then it has become an active participant in the restoration, promotion and operation of the line.

**For further information, see the association's website:
http://volkselectricrailway.co.uk**

ELECTRICS OF THE 50s

▲1041 081-1 in the former standard red ÖBB livery heads a freight through Stainach-Irdning on 09/09/87.
Peter Fox

▼The Class 1141 is a higher speed development of the 1041, having a top speed of 110 km/h instead of 80 km/h. 1141 029-7 is seen at Zell am See at the head of the 13.27 to Villach. *Ian Futers*

ELECTRICS INTO THE 70s

▲The standard mixed traffic electric locomotives of the 60s and 70s was the 1042 of which 168 were built. 1042 017-2 is seen at Eisenerz at the head of an iron ore train on 09/09/87.　　*Peter Fox*

▼The 1043s were delivered from 1971–73 as thyristor control prototypes. They were identical to the SJ class Rc2 even being delivered in SJ livery! 1043 001-5 is seen at the Wien Nord exhibition on 03/10/87.　　*Bevan Price*

▲Class 1045 dates from 1927 and the survivors are used on local freights and pilot duties, as are classes 1145 and 1245. 1045.09 was restored to original livery for the 1987 celebrations and is seen at the Wien Nord show on 03/10/88. *Bevan Price*

▼The second development of Class 1045 is the 1245. 1245 519-2 is seen on pilot duties at Villach Hbf during Feb 89. *John Stein*

FROM LOCAL DUTIES TO EURO-CITY

▲Vehicles of class 1046 were formerly classified as electric railcars (4061) and are, in fact motor luggage vans. 1046 016-0 is about to leave Hieflau with the 11.35 Amstetten–Selzthal on 09/09/87.　　*Peter Fox*

▼Two class 1046s have been rebuilt to dual-voltage locos as class 1146 for working the EuroCity trains 'Lehar' between Wien and Budapest. 1146 001-1 is seen at the Wien Nord exhibition on 03/10/87 in the new ÖBB livery.　　*Brian Garvin*

SHUNTING CURIOSITIES

▲The Class 1061 is a jackshaft-driven eight-coupled shunter dating from 1926. 1061 005-3 is seen on station pilot duties at Innsbruck on 10/02/88. *Graham Scott-Lowe*

▼The 1161 is the later development with minor detail variations. 1161 006-0 is seen at the same location on 10/08/88. *David Benyon*

MODERN SHUNTING & TRIP WORKING LOCOS

▲Two modern classes of loco for shunting and trip working have been delivered in recent years, the 1063 and 1064. 1063 013-5 is seen on pilot duties at Innsbruck on 10/08/88. *David Benyon*

▼The 1064 is the heavier duty version, being a Co–Co instead of a Bo–Bo. 1064 003-5 is seen as yard pilot at Villach West on 22/08/86, before its computer number was applied. *Brian Garvin*

ANCIENT TEN-COUPLERS

▲Class 1080 and the slightly more powerful 1180 are in the process of withdrawal. 1080 002-7 in faded green livery is seen shunting iron ore wagons at Eisenerz on 09/09/87. *Peter Fox*

▼1180 003-9 is seen inside Bludenz depot on 18/09/86. *Peter Heppenstall*

DIESEL & ELECTRIC ODDITIES

▲1067 004-0 is one of two survivors of a most unusual type of loco, an electric-hydraulic. It is shown in Selzthal shed yard on 09/09/87.
Peter Fox

▼The strange centre-cab class 2045 diesel-electrics date from the early fifties and featured steam heating. 2045.20, specially repainted in original green livery is seen in the 150th anniversary parade at Strasshof on 13/09/87.
Peter Fox

MAIN-LINE DIESEL-HYDRAULICS

▲The two standard classes of main-line diesels are classes 2043 and 2143, both of which fulfil the same specification. Class 2043 is built by Jenbacher Werke and 2043 067-6 is seen ex-works in the new livery at Zeltweg on 13/10/88. *Peter Heppenstall*

▼Class 2143 is built by SGP. 2143 021-0 is seen on a passenger train at Kernhof on 04/11/86. *Philip Wormald*

DIESEL SHUNTERS & SNOWPLOUGHS

▲The smallest diesel shunter on the ÖBB is the 2060. 2060 027-6 stands at Hieflau on 09/09/87.
Peter Fox

▼This self-propelled snowplough No. 2180 001-6 was one of the stars of the Strasshof parade on 13/09/87.
Peter Fox

TRANSALPIN UNITS ON PARADE

▲The original 'Transalpin' units were the class 4130, now reduced to local duties. A four-car set consisting of 4130.01/7130.02/7130.03/6130.01 was repainted in original livery for the 1987 celebrations   *Peter Fox*

▼Class 4010 were the successors to the 4130s on the Transalpin service, but they have now been replaced by loco-hauled stock. They are now used on Express services all over Austria. Set 4010 025-7 is shown here.
                                                                                                                    Peter Fox

SECONDARY UNITS

▲Three car EMU 4030 210 repainted in original livery. These units can be seen on secondary services in various parts of Austria. *Peter Fox*

▼The only survivor of class 5042 is 5042.14, restored now as active museum stock as VT 4214. It is still officially regarded as capital stock and can therefore work service trains. *Peter Fox*

DIESEL RAILCARS & TRAILERS

▲Class 5145 is allocated entirely to Wien Ost depot. On 13/09/87, 5145 012-0 with driving trailer 6545 011-6 were employed on a shuttle service to the WO depot open day. *Peter Fox*

▼These old four-wheeled open-balconied coaches modified with oil heaters are often used as trailers for diesel railcars. 50 81 24-19 008-5 is seen coupled to a two car 5146/6546 combination on the 13.25 St. Pölten–Leobersdorf on 14/09/87. *Peter Fox*

DIESEL RAILBUSES

▲The ÖBB has a number of DRBs which are similar to the DB class 798, but they are rapidly being phased out. This photograph shows a three-car combination in the Strasshof Parade headed by 5081 011-8.

Peter Fox

▼Four DRB trailers of class 7081 have been modified to act as trailers to relieve overcrowding on the new class 5047 units. 7047 002-6 is seen at St. Valentin on 07/10/88. *Peter Heppenstall*

NARROW-GAUGE SHUNTERS

▲2090 001-5 is the only member of its class, and can usually be found shunting at Waidhofen a.d. Ybbs, as it was on 29/09/87.
Bevan Price

▼Survivors from the second world war, class 2092 can be found shunting on three narrow-gauge systems. 2092 004-7 is seen in the shed yard at Gmünd on 12/09/87.
Peter Fox

NARROW-GAUGE IN TRANSITION

▲Class 2091 No. 2091 011-3 arrives at Gross Hollenstein on 29/09/87 with the 09.37 Kienberg Gaming–Waidhofen a.d. Ybbs whilst 0–6–4T 598.02 (owned by 'Club 598') and numbered Yv2 crosses with an LCGB charter special from Waidhofen to Kienberg Gaming. The line from Kienberg Gaming to Lunz am See has since been closed.
Bevan Price

▼The new order for the narrow gauge is the class 5090 diesel railcar. 5090 002-6 and 5090 001-8 are seen at Zell am See on 01/08/86.
John Stein

Seats: 56S + 64S 2L + 64S.
Weight: 62 + 33 + 34 tonnes.
Length over Buffers: 23.30 + 22.8 + 23.3 m.
Max. Speed: 120 km/h.

4020 001-6 7020 001-9 6020 001-1 S	WF	4020 061-0 7020 061-3 6020 061-5 S	FD
4020 002-4 7020 002-7 6020 002-9 S	WF	4020 062-8 7020 062-1 6020 062-3 S	FD
4020 003-2 7020 003-5 6020 003-7 S	WF	4020 063-6 7020 063-9 6020 063-1 S	FD
4020 004-0 7020 004-3 6020 004-5 S	WF	4020 064-4 7020 064-7 6020 064-9 S	FD
4020 005-7 7020 005-0 6020 005-2 S	FD	4020 065-1 7020 065-4 6020 065-6 S	FD
4020 006-5 7020 006-8 6020 006-0 S	FD	4020 066-9 7020 066-2 6020 066-4 S	FD
4020 007-3 7020 007-6 6020 007-8 S	FD	4020 067-7 7020 067-0 6020 067-2 S	FD
4020 008-1 7020 008-4 6020 008-6 S	FD	4020 068-5 7020 068-8 6020 068-0 S	FD
4020 009-9 7020 009-2 6020 009-4 S	FD	4020 069-3 7020 069-6 6020 069-8 S	FD
4020 010-7 7020 010-0 6020 010-2 S	FD	4020 070-1 7020 070-4 6020 070-6 S	BL
4020 011-5 7020 011-8 6020 011-0 S	FD	4020 071-9 7020 071-2 6020 071-4 S	BL
4020 012-3 7020 012-6 6020 012-8 S	FD	4020 072-7 7020 072-0 6020 072-2 S	BL
4020 013-1 7020 013-4 6020 013-6 S	FD	4020 073-5 7020 073-8 6020 073-0 S	FD
4020 014-9 7020 014-2 6020 014-4 S	FD	4020 074-3 7020 074-6 6020 074-8 S	FD
4020 015-6 7020 015-9 6020 015-1 S	FD	4020 075-0 7020 075-3 6020 075-5 S	FD
4020 016-4 7020 016-7 6020 016-9 S	FD	4020 076-8 7020 076-1 6020 076-3 S	FD
4020 017-2 7020 017-5 6020 017-7 S	FD	4020 077-6 7020 077-9 6020 077-1 S	FD
4020 018-0 7020 018-3 6020 018-5 S	FD	4020 078-4 7020 078-7 6020 078-9 S	FD
4020 019-8 7020 019-1 6020 019-3 S	FD	4020 079-2 7020 079-5 6020 079-7 S	FD
4020 020-6 7020 020-9 6020 020-1 S	FD	4020 080-0 7020 080-3 6020 080-5 S	LZ
4020 021-4 7020 021-7 6020 021-9 S	FD	4020 081-8 7020 081-1 6020 081-3 S	LZ
4020 022-2 7020 022-5 6020 022-7 S	FD	4020 082-6 7020 082-9 6020 082-1 S	LZ
4020 023-0 7020 023-3 6020 023-5 S	FD	4020 083-4 7020 083-7 6020 083-9 S	LZ
4020 024-8 7020 024-1 6020 024-3 S	FD	4020 084-2 7020 084-5 6020 084-7 S	LZ
4020 025-5 7020 025-8 6020 025-0 S	FD	4020 085-9 7020 085-2 6020 085-4 S	FD
4020 026-3 7020 026-6 6020 026-8 S	FD	4020 086-7 7020 086-0 6020 086-2 S	FD
4020 027-1 7020 027-4 6020 027-6 S	FD	4020 087-5 7020 087-8 6020 087-0 S	FD
4020 028-9 7020 028-2 6020 028-4 S	FD	4020 088-3 7020 088-6 6020 088-8 S	FD
4020 029-7 7020 029-0 6020 029-2 S	FD	4020 089-1 7020 089-4 6020 089-6 S	FD
4020 030-5 7020 030-8 6020 030-0 S	FD	4020 090-9 7020 090-2 6020 090-4 S	FD
4020 031-3 7020 031-6 6020 031-8 S	FD	4020 091-7 7020 091-0 6020 091-2 S	FD
4020 032-1 7020 032-4 6020 032-6 S	FD	4020 092-5 7020 092-8 6020 092-0 S	FD
4020 033-9 7020 033-2 6020 033-4 S	FD	4020 093-3 7020 093-6 6020 093-8 S	FD
4020 034-7 7020 034-0 6020 034-2 S	FD	4020 094-1 7020 094-4 6020 094-6 S	FD
4020 035-4 7020 035-7 6020 035-9 S	FD	4020 095-8 7020 095-1 6020 095-3 S	WF
4020 036-2 7020 036-5 6020 036-7 S	FD	4020 096-6 7020 096-9 6020 096-1 S	WF
4020 037-0 7020 037-3 6020 037-5 S	FD	4020 097-4 7020 097-7 6020 097-9 S	WF
4020 038-8 7020 038-1 6020 038-3 S	FD	4020 098-2 7020 098-5 6020 098-7 S	WF
4020 039-6 7020 039-9 6020 039-1 S	FD	4020 099-0 7020 099-3 6020 099-5 S	WF
4020 040-4 7020 040-7 6020 040-9 S	FD	4020 100-6 7020 100-9 6020 100-1 S	WF
4020 041-2 7020 041-5 6020 041-7 S	FD	4020 101-4 7020 101-7 6020 101-9 S	BL
4020 042-0 7020 042-3 6020 042-5 S	FD	4020 102-2 7020 102-5 6020 102-7 S	BL
4020 043-8 7020 043-1 6020 043-3 S	FD	4020 103-0 7020 103-3 6020 103-5 S	BL
4020 044-6 7020 044-9 6020 044-1 S	FD	4020 104-8 7020 104-1 6020 104-3 S	BL
4020 045-3 7020 045-6 6020 045-8 S	FD	4020 105-5 7020 105-8 6020 105-0 S	BL
4020 046-1 7020 046-4 6020 046-6 S	FD	4020 106-3 7020 106-6 6020 106-8 S	BL
4020 047-9 7020 047-2 6020 047-4 S	FD	4020 107-1 7020 107-4 6020 107-6 S	IN
4020 048-7 7020 048-0 6020 048-2 S	FD	4020 108-9 7020 108-2 6020 108-4 S	IN
4020 049-5 7020 049-8 6020 049-0 S	FD	4020 109-7 7020 109-0 6020 109-2 S	IN
4020 050-3 7020 050-6 6020 050-8 S	FD	4020 110-5 7020 110-8 6020 110-0 S	IN
4020 051-1 7020 051-4 6020 051-6 S	FD	4020 111-3 7020 111-6 6020 111-8 S	IN
4020 052-9 7020 052-2 6020 052-4 S	WF	4020 112-1 7020 112-4 6020 112-6 S	FD
4020 053-7 7020 053-0 6020 053-2 S	WF	4020 113-9 7020 113-2 6020 113-4 S	FD
4020 054-0 7020 054-8 6020 054-0 S	WF	4020 114-7 7020 114-0 6020 114-2 S	FD
4020 055-2 7020 055-5 6020 055-7 S	WF	4020 115-4 7020 115-7 6020 115-9 S	FD
4020 056-0 7020 056-3 6020 056-5 S	IN	4020 116-2 7020 116-5 6020 116-7 S	FD
4020 057-8 7020 057-1 6020 057-3 S	IN	4020 117-0 7020 117-3 6020 117-5 S	FD
4020 058-6 7020 058-9 6020 058-1 S	IN	4020 118-8 7020 118-1 6020 118-3 S	FD
4020 059-4 7020 059-7 6020 059-9 S	IN	4020 119-6 7020 119-9 6020 119-1 S	FD
4020 060-2 7020 060-5 6020 060-7 S	FD	4020 120-4 7020 120-7 6020 120-9 S	FD

In S-bahn livery, 4020 107-1 is seen at Stans bei Schwaz during August 1986.

John Stein

CLASS 4030.1   3-CAR UNITS

These units work from Wien FJB to Krems & St.Pölten.

B4hET + B4hTl + BD4hES (DMSO–TSO–DTBSO).

Built: 1960.
Builder-Mech Parts: Simmering-Graz-Pauker.

Builder-Elec. Parts: Brown-Boveri/Elin.
Traction Motors: 4 x 250 kW.
Seats: 72S + 72S 1L + 56S.
Weight: 65 + 36 + 37 tonnes.
Length over Buffers: 23.19 + 22.59 + 23.54 m.
Max. Speed: 100 km/h.

4030 101-2 7030 101-5 6030 101-7 **E**	WF	
4030 102-0 7030 102-3 6030 102-5 **E**	WF	

4030 103-8 7030 103-1 6030 103-3 **E**	WF	
4030 104-6 7030 104-9 6030 104-1 **E**	WF	

CLASS 4030.2   3-CAR UNITS

These units were built for suburban services around Wien but some have now been transferred to Linz and Salzburg. Those in Wien are fitted with Scharfenberg couplings. They are found on local passenger trains in the Wien area taking in Hegyeshalom and Wiener Neustadt amongst other places, whilst the Wien FJB units also work to Krems & St.Pölten. Those at Linz see use on the Summerau line and sometimes between Hieflau and Eisenerz. The Salzburg units work to Attnang-Puchheim, Schladming and Saalfelden. The Villach units work local services on the routes radiating from there getting as far away as Leoben. 4030 210 was restored to old S-Bahn livery for the 1987 Celebrations.

B4hET + B4hTl + BD4hES (DMSO–TSO–DTBSO).

Built: 1961–66 (1970–75*).
Builder-Mech Parts: Simmering-Graz-Pauker.
Builder-Elec. Parts: Brown-Boveri/Elin.
Traction Motors: 4 x 250 kW.
Seats: 76S + 72S 1L + 58S 1L (66S 1L*).
Weight: 56 + 33 + 32 tonnes.
Length over Buffers: 23.50 + 22.99 + 23.50 m.
Max. Speed: 100 km/h.

4030 201-0 7030 201-3 6030 201-5 **E**	WF	4030 224-2 7030 224-5 6030 224-7 **E**		LZ
4030 202-8 7030 202-1 6030 202-3 **E**	WF	4030 225-9 7030 225-2 6030 225-4 **E**		LZ
4030 203-6 7030 203-9 6030 203-1 **E**	WF	4030 226-7 7030 226-0 6030 226-2 **E**	*	VH
4030 204-4 7030 204-7 6030 204-9 **E**	WF	4030 227-5 7030 227-8 6030 227-0 **E**	*	VH
4030 205-1 7030 205-4 6030 205-6 **E**	WF	4030 228-3 7030 228-6 6030 228-8 **E**	*	VH
4030 206-9 7030 206-2 6030 206-4 **E**	WF	4030 229-1 7030 229-4 6030 229-6 **E**	*	VH
4030 207-7 7030 207-0 6030 207-2 **E**	WF	4030 230-9 7030 230-2 6030 230-4 **E**	*	VH
4030 208-5 7030 208-8 6030 208-0 **E**	WF	4030 231-7 7030 231-0 6030 231-2 **E**	*	VH
4030 209-3 7030 209-6 6030 209-8 **E**	FD	4030 232-5 7030 232-8 6030 232-0 **E**	*	SB
4030 210-1 7030 210-4 6030 210-6 **O**	FD	4030 233-3 7030 233-6 6030 233-8 **E**	*	SB
4030 211-9 7030 211-2 6030 211-4 **E**	FD	4030 234-1 7030 234-4 6030 234-6 **E**	*	SB
4030 212-7 7030 212-0 6030 212-2 **E**	FD	4030 235-8 7030 235-1 6030 235-3 **E**	*	WF
4030 213-5 7030 213-8 6030 213-0 **E**	FD	4030 236-6 7030 236-9 6030 236-1 **E**	*	WF
4030 214-3 7030 214-6 6030 214-8 **E**	FD	4030 237-4 7030 237-7 6030 237-9 **E**	*	WF
4030 215-0 7030 215-3 6030 215-5 **E**	FD	4030 238-2 7030 238-5 6030 238-7 **E**	*	WF
4030 216-8 7030 216-1 6030 216-3 **E**	FD	4030 239-0 7030 239-3 6030 239-5 **E**	*	WF
4030 217-6 7030 217-9 6030 217-1 **E**	FD	4030 240-8 7030 240-1 6030 240-3 **E**	*	SB
4030 218-4 7030 218-7 6030 218-9 **E**	FD	4030 241-6 7030 241-9 6030 241-1 **E**	*	SB
4030 219-2 7030 219-5 6030 219-7 **E**	FD	4030 242-4 7030 242-7 6030 242-9 **E**	*	SB
4030 220-0 7030 220-3 6030 220-5 **E**	FD	4030 243-2 7030 243-5 6030 243-7 **E**	*	SB
4030 221-8 7030 221-1 6030 221-3 **E**	LZ	4030 244-0 7030 244-3 6030 244-5 **E**	*	SB
4030 222-6 7030 222-9 6030 222-1 **E**	LZ	4030 245-7 7030 245-0 6030 245-2 **E**	*	SB
4030 223-4 7030 223-7 6030 223-9 **E**	LZ	4030 246-5 7030 246-8 6030 246-0 **E**	*	SB

CLASS 4030.3   2/3/4-CAR UNITS

This class originated as cl. 4030.0. Although sliding doors were fitted they were not power operated. All have now been modified and reclassified to work in multiple. Built as 4-car units most now operate as 3-car and in some cases 2-car units. The spare trailers are used for strengthening when required or in Wien as loco hauled stock behind cl. 1046 (which used to be classed as electric railcars anyway), and with class 4130. All fitted with screw couplings. Use: Wien area as for cl. 4030.1. Innsbruck units work locals to Reutte, Kufstein and Landeck whilst those at Bludenz are on locals to Bregenz, Lindau, Buchs and St.Margarethen. The Villach units work local services on lines radiating from Villach and 2–car units also get as far as the newly electrified line to Vordernberg Markt.

B4hET + 2B4hTl + BD4hES (DMSO–2TSO–DTBSO) [as built].

Built: 1956–59.
Builder-Mech Parts: Simmering-Graz-Pauker.
Builder-Elec. Parts: Brown-Boveri/AEG/Elin.
Traction Motors: 4 x 250 kW.
Seats: 72S 1L + 72S + 56S 1L.
Weight: 68 + 36 + 37 tonnes.
Length over Buffers: 23.19 + 22.59 + 23.54 m.
Max. Speed: 100 km/h.

4030 301-8 7030 301-1 6030 301-3 **E**	IN		4030 312-5 7030 312-8 6030 312-0 **E**	IN
4030 302-6 7030 302-9 6030 302-1 **E**	IN		4030 313-3 7030 313-6 6030 313-8 **E**	IN
4030 303-4 7030 303-7 6030 303-9 **E**	WF		4030 314-1 7030 314-4 6030 314-6 **E**	WF
4030 304-2 7030 304-5 6030 304-7 **E**	WF		4030 315-8 7030 315-1 6030 315-3 **E**	VH
4030 305-9 7030 305-2 6030 305-4 **E**	VH		4030 316-6 7030 316-9 6030 316-1 **E**	IN
4030 306-7 7030 306-0 6030 306-2 **E**	WF		4030 317-4 7030 317-7 6030 317-9 **E**	VH
4030 307-5 7030 307-8 6030 307-0 **E**	IN		4030 318-2 7030 318-5 6030 318-7 **E**	BL
4030 308-3 7030 308-6 6030 308-8 **E**	IN		4030 319-0 7030 319-3 6030 319-5 **E**	VH
4030 309-1 7030 309-4 6030 309-6 **E**	BL		4030 320-8 7030 320-1 6030 320-3 **E**	VH
4030 310-9 7030 310-2 6030 310-4 **E**	BL		4030 321-6 7030 321-9 6030 321-1 **E**	IN
4030 311-7 7030 311-0 6030 311-2 **E**	IN		4030 322-4 7030 322-7 6030 322-9 **E**	WF

Spare TSO. 72S. 36 t. 22.59 m.

7030 323-5 **E**	WN		7030 332-6 **E**	VH		7030 341-7 **E**	WN
7030 324-3 **E**	WN		7030 333-4 **E**	WN		7030 342-5 **E**	WN
7030 325-0 **E**	WN		7030 334-2 **E**	VH		7030 343-3 **E**	WN
7030 326-8 **E**	LZ		7030 335-9 **E**	VH		7030 344-1 **E**	WN
7030 327-6 **E**	WN		7030 336-7 **E**	WN		7030 345-8 **E**	WN
7030 328-4 **E**	WN		7030 337-5 **E**	WN		7030 346-6 **E**	WN
7030 329-2 **E**	WN		7030 338-3 **E**	LZ		7030 347-4 **E**	WN
7030 330-0 **E**	VH		7030 339-1 **E**	WN		7030 348-2 **E**	WN
7030 331-8 **E**	VH		7030 340-9 **E**	WN			

CLASS 4130   3/4-CAR UNITS

These units were built as 4-car units for use on the Transalpin service. When replaced by cl. 4010 they saw use around Wien for a time. Now they are all based in Villach for services to Rosenbach and St.Veit a.d. Glan. 4130.03 was involved in a crash and has been withdrawn. The remaining units are running with class 7030 trailers with the 7130 trailers being used as hauled stock. One set was restored to Transalpin livery for the 1987 Celebrations, whilst another has been sold to the Montafonerbahn.

B4hET + 2B4hTl + BD4hES (DMSO–2TSK–DTBSO) [as built].

Built: 1958.
Builder-Mech Parts: Simmering-Graz-Pauker.
Builder-Elec. Parts: Siemens/Brown Boveri.
Traction Motors: 4 x 315 kW.
Max. Speed: 130 km/h.

DMSO. 62S. 69.6 t. 23.19 m.

4130 001-3 **T**	VH	4130 004-7 **E**	VH

TSK. 48S. 37 t. 22.59 m. Now mainly used as hauled stock.

7130 002-4 **T**	VH	7130 005-7 **E**	VH	7130 101-4 **E**	VH
7130 003-2 **T**	VH	7130 006-5 **E**	VH	7130 102-2 **E**	VH
7130 004-0 **E**	VH				

DTBSO. 56S. 37 t. 23.54 m.

6130 001-8 **T**	VH	6130 003-4 **E**	VH	6130 004-2 **E**	VH

DIESEL RAILCARS

Note: All bogie diesel railcars have the wheel arrangement B–2 except for class 5042 which is 1A–A1.

CLASS 5042 SINGLE CARS

The last survivor of a class of 14 built for Wien suburban services before electrification. It was restored to original livery for the 1987 Celebrations and is now regarded as active museum stock.

B4VT (DMSO).

Built: 1937.
Builder: Simmering.
Engine: Two Simmering R8 of 155 kW.
Transmission: Electric.
Seats: 78S 1L.
Weight: 56.8 tonnes.
Length over Buffers: 22.44 m.
Max. Speed: 110 km/h.

5042 014-0 **D**　WN

CLASS 5144 SINGLE CARS

Line closures north of Wien have left this class with few duties.One unit covers all trains on the Siebenbrunn–Engelhartstetten line whilst another is subshedded at Hohenau for use on staff and school trains in that area.

B4VT (DMSO).

Built: 1951.
Builder: Simmering.
Engine:Simmering R12a of 310 kW.
Transmission: Hydraulic.
Seats: 64S 1L.
Weight: 53.5 tonnes.
Length over Buffers: 23.52 m.
Max. Speed: 115 km/h.

5144 001-4 **D**　WN	5144 004-8 **D**　WN	5144 005-5 **D**　WN
5144 003-0 **D**　WN		

CLASS 5145/6545/6645 2–CAR UNITS

Built as long distance DMUs for fast services when most lines were still steam worked these units are now only used on local services. Their sphere of operation is Gänserndorf–Marchegg, Wien Süd (Ostseite)–Wiener Neustadt/Eisenstadt/Wulkaprodersdorf/ Sopron but some of these workings will change to 5047 in late 1988/early 1989.

B4VT + B4VS (DMSO–DTSO). Class 5145 sometimes work as single cars.

Built: 1952–7.
Builder: Simmering.
Engine: SGP S 12a of 400 kW.
Transmission: Hydraulic.
Seats: 56S 1L + 80S 1L (64S 1L*).
Weight: 47.3 + 28.2 (28.9*) tonnes.
Length over Buffers: 21.85 + 21.85 m.
Max. Speed: 115 km/h.

5145 001-3 6545 001-7	**D**	WO	5145 007-0 6545 007-4	**D**	WO
5145 002-1 6545 002-5	**D**	WO	5145 008-8 6545 004-1	**D**	WO
5145 003-9 6645 001-6	**D** *	WO	5145 009-6 6545 009-0	**D**	WO
5145 004-7 6545 003-3	**D**	WO	5145 010-4 6545 010-8	**D**	WO
5145 005-4 6545 005-8	**D**	WO	5145 011-2 6545 011-6	**D**	WO
5145 006-2 6545 006-6	**D**	WO	5145 012-0 6545 012-4	**D**	WO

Driving trailer 6546 204-6 is seen paired with diesel-hydraulic railcar 5046 204-3 at Wiener Neustadt on 15/09/87 with an evening train to Aspang.

Colin Boocock

5145 013-8 6545 008-2	**D** WO	5145 015-3 6645 003-2	**D** * WO		
5145 014-6 6645 002-4	**D** * WO	5145 016-1 6645 004-0	**D** * WO		

Class 7645. AB4TI (CK). Seats: 30F 31S 1L. Weight: 28 tonnes. Length: 21.80 m. These vehicles were built as DMU trailers, but are now usually used as hauled stock.

5145 001-3 **D**	WO	5145 014-6 **D**	WO	6545 011-6 **D**	WO
5145 002-1 **D**	WO	5145 015-3 **D**	WO	6545 012-4 **D**	WO
5145 003-9 **D**	WO	5145 016-1 **D**	WO	6645 001-6 **D**	WO
5145 004-7 **D**	WO	6545 001-7 **D**	WO	6645 002-4 **D**	WO
5145 005-4 **D**	WO	6545 002-5 **D**	WO	6645 003-2 **D**	WO
5145 006-2 **D**	WO	6545 003-3 **D**	WO	6645 004-0 **D**	WO
5145 007-0 **D**	WO	6545 004-1 **D**	WO	7645 001-4 **D**	WO
5145 008-8 **D**	WO	6545 005-8 **D**	WO	7645 002-2 **D**	WO
5145 009-6 **D**	WO	6545 006-6 **D**	WO	7645 003-0 **D**	WO
5145 010-4 **D**	WO	6545 007-4 **D**	WO	7645 004-8 **D**	WO
5145 011-2 **D**	WO	6545 008-2 **D**	WO	7645 005-5 **D**	WO
5145 012-0 **D**	WO	6545 009-0 **D**	WO	7645 006-3 **D**	WO
5145 013-8 **D**	WO	6545 010-8 **D**	WO		

Class 7845. AR4TI (RF). Seats: 18F 1L. Weight: 34.9 tonnes. Length: 21.81 m. These vehicles were built as DMU trailers, but are now usually used as hauled stock.

7845 001-2 **D**	WO	7845 002-0 **D**	WO	7845 003-8 **D**	WO

CLASS 5046/5146/6546   SINGLE CARS

Class 5046 was based on the cl. 5145 but intended for secondary duties. Recently rebuilt with warm air heating and fitted for multiple working. Cl. 5146 is similar to cl. 5046 but with a more powerful engine. Class 6546 are driving trailers, of which some have recently been converted from hauled stock. There are no fixed formations.

Use is as follows:

GZ Spielfeld Strass–Bad Radkersburg, and Fehring area.
KD Wolfsberg–St.Paul–Lavemünd, Zeltweg–Fohnsdorf, St.Veit a.d.Glan–Hüttenberg, Klagenfurt–Rosenbach.
NS Wiener Neustadt–Gutenstein/Aspang/Puchberg.
SP Branches to Türnitz, Markt St.Agyd, also Pöchlarn–Kienberg Gaming, and St.Pölten–Krems–St.Valentin.

Built: 1954–5 (5046), 1959–61 (5146), 1955–88 (6546).
Builder: Simmering-Graz-Pauker.
Engine: SGP S 12a of 370 kW (5046), 400 kW (5146).
Transmission: Hydraulic.
Max. Speed: 100 km/h.

Class 5046. BD4VT (DMBSO). Seats: 48S 1L. Weight: 50 tonnes. Length: 24.71 m.

5046 201-9 **D**	NS	5046 207-6 **D**	NS	5046 213-4 **D**	KD
5046 202-7 **D**	NS	5046 208-4 **D**	NS	5046 214-2 **D**	KD
5046 203-5 **D**	NS	5046 209-2 **D**	GZ	5046 215-9 **D**	NS
5046 204-3 **D**	NS	5046 210-0 **D**	GZ	5046 216-7 **D**	SP
5046 205-0 **D**	NS	5046 211-8 **D**	GZ	5046 217-5 **D**	SP
5046 206-8 **D**	NS	5046 212-6 **D**	KD		

Class 5146. BD4VT (DMBSO). Seats: 48S 1L. Weight: 51 tonnes. Length: 24.71 m.

5146 201-8 **D**	SP	5146 204-2 **D**	SP	5146 207-5 **D**	KD
5146 202-6 **D**	SP	5146 205-9 **D**	SP	5146 208-3 **D**	KD
5146 203-4 **D**	KD	5146 206-7 **D**	SP		

Class 6546. B4VS (DTSO). Seats: 80S 1L. Weight: 29 tonnes. Length: 23.03 m.

6546 201-2 **D**	NS	6546 208-7 **D**	NS	6546 215-2 **D**	NS
6546 202-0 **D**	NS	6546 209-5 **D**	GZ	6546 216-0 **D**	SP
6546 203-8 **D**	NS	6546 210-3 **D**	GZ	6546 217-8 **D**	SP
6546 204-6 **D**	NS	6546 211-1 **D**	GZ	6546 218-6 **D**	SP
6546 205-3 **D**	NS	6546 212-9 **D**	KD	6546 219-4 **D**	SP
6546 206-1 **D**	NS	6546 213-7 **D**	KD	6546 220-2 **D**	SP
6546 207-9 **D**	NS	6546 214-5 **D**	KD	6546 221-0 **D**	SP

| 6546 222-8 **D** | SP | 6546 224-4 **D** | SP | 6546 226-9 **D** | SP |
| 6546 223-6 **D** | SP | 6546 225-1 **D** | SP | | |

Note: Various other vehicles were built as diesel railcar trailers, but these are mainly used these days as hauled stock. These are classes 7758 (4 vehicles), 7759 (7 vehicles). There are also a number of 4-wheeled coaches of particularly antiquated appearance which were converted to oil heating and are also used as railcar trailers, but these are also often to be seen as guard's vans on freight trains these days and have been renumbered into the coaching stock series (50 81 24-09 and 50 81 24-19 series.

CLASS 5047/7047

Introduced 1987 the class 5047 features modern seating as in the latest main line stock. The units are intended for branch line use under driver only operation. The driver issues tickets to those passengers joining and the internal door to the cab has been designed to act as a ticket office window also with a slot for money/tickets to be exchanged. Fitted with PA and doors controlled by the driver. Hydrodynamic braking. The new units have been so successful in attracting new business on some of the branch lines that some trailers have had to be hurriedly provided. In addition, certain closed lines may be reopened! Class 7047 is a rebuilt 7081. Interior seating is as in the 5047 whilst new wiring allows the driver to operate lights, PA and doors from the 5047. Class 6547 driving trailers have now also been ordered for delivery 4–11/90.

Used as follows:

KR Waidhofen a.d. Thaya–Schwarzenau–Zwettl, Sigmundsherberg–Krems–St.Pölten.
WO Gänserndorf–Gross Schweinbarth–Obersdorf, Drösing–Zisterdorf Stadt, Neusiedl–Pamhagen, Neusiedl–Wulkaprodersdorf–Deutschkreutz. (More duties in this area in 1989)
WE Wels will get some units in 1988/89 to replace 5081s.

Built: 1987.
Builder: Jenbacher Werke.
Engine: Daimler Benz OM444LA 419 kW.
Transmission: Hydraulic.
Seats: 62S 1L plus 6 pull down.
Weight:
Length over Buffers: 25.42 m.
Max. Speed: 120 km/h.

Class 5047. BD4VT (DMSO).

5047 001-2 **C**	KR	5047 012-9 **C**	WE	5047 023-6 **C**	
5047 002-0 **C**	KR	5047 013-7 **C**	WO	5047 024-4 **C**	
5047 003-8 **C**	KR	5047 014-5 **C**	WO	5047 025-1 **C**	
5047 004-6 **C**	KR	5047 015-2 **C**	WO	5047 026-9 **C**	
5047 005-3 **C**	KR	5047 016-0 **C**	WO	5047 027-7 **C**	
5047 006-1 **C**	KR	5047 017-8 **C**	WO	5047 028-5 **C**	
5047 007-9 **C**	KR	5047 018-6 **C**	WO	5047 029-3 **C**	
5047 008-7 **C**	KR	5047 019-4 **C**	WO	5047 030-1 **C**	
5047 009-5 **C**	KR	5047 020-2 **C**	WO	5047 031-9 **C**	
5047 010-3 **C**	KR	5047 021-0 **C**		5047 032-7 **C**	
5047 011-1 **C**	WE	5047 022-8 **C**			

Class 6547. B4ES (DTSO) (on order).

6547 001-5 **C**	6547 007-2 **C**	6547 012-2 **C**
6547 002-3 **C**	6547 008-0 **C**	6547 013-0 **C**
6547 003-1 **C**	6547 009-8 **C**	6547 014-8 **C**
6547 004-9 **C**	6547 010-6 **C**	6547 015-5 **C**
6547 005-6 **C**	6547 011-4 **C**	6547 016-3 **C**
6547 006-4 **C**		

Class 7047. BTI (TSO). Seats: 40S 1L. Weight: 11 tonnes. Length: 13.95 m.

| 7047 001-8 (7081 013-0) **C** | KR | 7047 003-4 (7081 005-6) **C** | KR |
| 7047 002-6 (7081 014-8) **C** | KR | 7047 004-2 (7081 006-4) **C** | KR |

CLASS 5081/6581/7081
4w RAILBUSES & TRAILERS

Class 5081 is a lightweight railbus based on the DB cl. 798. Now being progressively replaced by the new cl. 5047. Surprisingly some 7081s were rebuilt to cl.7047. The 5081 5xx series units have special modifications for the steeply graded line from Vordernberg. This line closed in 1988 and the units are unlikely to be converted back to normal as they have a limited future. Class 6581 is a driving trailer whilst 7081 is an intermediate trailer. There are no fixed formations.

Use:
MZ Neuberg branch trains
WE Wels – Aschach/Braunau/Grünau, Attnang Puchheim – Schärding, Steindorf – Braunau.

Built: 1964–67.
Builders: Uerdingen/Jenbacher Werke/Simmering-Graz-Pauker.
Engine: Büssing U10.
Transmission: Mechanical.
Length over Buffers (5081): 13.95 m.
Max. Speed: 90 km/h.

Class 5081. BVT (DMSO). Seats: 56S 1L. Weight: 21 tonnes.

5081 001-9 **B**	MZ	5081 022-5 **B**	WE	5081 059-7 **B**	WE
5081 003-5 **B**	GZ	5081 051-4 **B**	WE	5081 560-4 **B**	WE
5081 015-9 **B**	WE	5081 052-2 **B**	WE	5081 561-2 **B**	KD
5081 016-7 **B**	WE	5081 053-0 **B**	WE	5081 562-0 **B**	KD
5081 019-1 **B**	WE	5081 055-5 **B**	WE	5081 563-8 **B**	WE
5081 021-7 **B**	WE	5081 057-1 **B**	WE	5081 565-3 **B**	WE

Class 6581. BDVS (DTBSO). Seats: 50S 1L. Weight: 11 tonnes.

6581 001-2 **B**	KD	6581 020-2 **B**	KD	6581 058-2 **B**	WE
6581 002-0 **B**	GZ	6581 051-7 **B**	KD	6581 061-6 **B**	WE
6581 003-8 **B**	GZ	6581 052-5 **B**	WE	6581 063-2 **B**	WE
6581 011-1 **B**	WE	6581 053-3 **B**	WE	6581 064-0 **B**	WE
6581 013-7 **B**	WE	6581 054-1 **B**	WE	6581 065-7 **B**	WE
6581 014-5 **B**	WE	6581 055-8 **B**	WE	6581 066-5 **B**	WE
6581 018-6 **B**	WE	6581 056-6 **B**	WE	6581 067-3 **B**	WE
6581 019-4 **B**	WE	6581 057-4 **B**	WE		

Class 7081. BTI (TSO). Seats: 63S 1L. Weight: 11 tonnes.

7081 004-9 **B**	WE	7081 018-9 **B**	WE	7081 026-2 **B**	KD
7081 007-2 **B**	WE	7081 019-7 **B**	WE	7081 027-0 **B**	KD
7081 008-0 **B**	WE	7081 021-3 **B**	WE	7081 051-0 **B**	WE
7081 009-8 **B**	WE	7081 022-1 **B**	WE	7081 052-8 **B**	WE
7081 011-4 **B**	WE	7081 023-9 **B**	WE	7081 053-6 **B**	WE
7081 016-3 **B**	WE	7081 024-7 **B**	WE	7081 054-4 **B**	WE
7081 017-1 **B**	WE				

NARROW GAUGE LOCOMOTIVES & RAILCARS

STEAM LOCOMOTIVES

Note: All steam locomotives are in black livery unless shown otherwise.

CLASS 298.2   0–6–2T

This two cylinder compound locomotive is the last of a class of three built for the Niederöster-reichischen Landesbahnen (NÖLB) for use on the line from St. Pölten to Mariazell. It has been based at Gmünd for many years for use on the narrow gauge network there. It is often used on passenger trains at weekends in the summer. The other two locos of the class are now preserved.

Built: 1905.
Builder: Krauss, Linz.
Gauge: 760 mm.
Driving Wheel Diameter: 800 mm.
Length over Couplings: 7.804 m.

Boiler Pressure: 1.28 MN/sq. m. (185 lb/sq.in).
Weight in Full Working Order: 27.5 tonnes.
Tractive Effort: 76.5 kN (17200lbf).
Cylinders (2): 320 x 400 mm, 500 x 400 mm.
Max. Speed: 35 km/h.

0298 207-2   GM

CLASS 399   0–8+4

These are Engerth type locomotives where the tender is articulated with the locomotive. So the wheel arrangement is shown as 0–8+4 although some 'experts' call them 0–8–4T! Like 298.207 they were built for the NÖLB Mariazell line and upon electrification and dieselisation of the lines from St. Pölten have congregated at Gmünd. The locomotives generally have no booked duties being spare to diesels (apart from summer weekend tourist trains on the line to Gross Gerungs), but actually see a lot of use. One loco is now based at Zell am See for tourist trains on the line to Krimml, whilst another is at St. Pölten for similar trains from there on the Mariazell and Gresten lines.

Built: 1906–08.
Builder: Krauss, Linz.
Gauge: 760 mm.
Driving Wheel Diameter: 900 mm.
Length over Couplings: 11.665 m.

Boiler Pressure: 1.28 MN/sq. m. (185 lb/sq.in).
Weight in Full Working Order: 45.1 tonnes.
Tractive Effort: 80.4 kN (18080 lbf).
Cylinders (2): 410 x 450 mm.
Max. Speed: 40 km/h.

0399 001-7	ZS	0399 003-3	GM	0399 005-8	GM
0399 002-5	GM	0399 004-1	GM	0399 006-6	SP

CLASSES 999.0 & 999.1   0–4–2RT

Class 999.0 were built for and continue to operate the rack line from Puchberg to Hochschneeberg (Schneebergbahn). Class 999.1 were all built for the Schafbergbahn, but one has been transferred to the Schneebergbahn to cover extra traffic there.

Built: 1893–94 (999.1), 1896–1900 (999.0).
Gauge: 1000 mm.
Boiler Pressure: 138 MN/sq. m. (200 lb/sq.in).
Builder: Krauss, Linz.
Weight in Full Working Order: 18.0 tonnes (999.0), 17.4 tonnes (999.1).
Length over Couplings: 5.55 m (999.0), 5.50 m (999.1).
Tractive Effort (Adhesion): 89.2 kN (20070 lbf). **(Rack):** 110.6 kN (24700 lbf).
Driving Wheel Diameter: 706 mm.   **Cylinders(2):** 320 x 600 mm.
Rack Wheel Diameter: 575 mm.   **Max. Speed:** 12 km/h.
Trailing Wheel Diameter: 520 mm.

Non-Standard Liveries: 0999 102/5 blue. 0999 104/6 green.

Class 999.0

0999 001-1	PB	0999 003-7	PB	0999 004-5	PB
0999 002-9	PB				

Class 999.1

0999 101-9	PB	Schneeberg	0999 104-3 **O**	SW	Bergprimel
0999 102-7 **O**	SW	Enzian	0999 105-0 **O**	SW	Almrausch
0999 103-5	SW	Erika	0999 106-8 **O**	SW	Berganemone

CLASS 999.2   0–4–2RT

New one-man-operated rack steam loco on order.

Built:
Gauge: 1000 mm.
Boiler Pressure: 157 MN/sq. m. (228 lb/sq.in).
Builder: SLM Winterthür.
Weight in Full Working Order:
Length over Couplings: 6.80 m.
Tractive Effort (Adhesion):   kN (lbf). **(Rack):**   kN (lbf).
Driving Wheel Diameter: mm.   **Cylinders (2):** 320 x 440 mm.
Rack Wheel Diameter: 573 mm.   **Max. Speed:** 12 km/h.
Trailing Wheel Diameter: mm.

0999 005-2	PB	0999 201-7	

ELECTRIC LOCOMOTIVES

CLASS 1099   C–C

Those narrow-gauge electric locos were rebodied in the 1960s and see service on the St. Pölten–Mariazell line. This line is well worth a visit to see these locomotives before they are replaced, as there is talk of new EMUs being ordered for the line.

Built: 1909–14.
Builder – Mech.Parts: Krauss.
Builder – Elec.Parts: Siemens-Wien.
Gauge: 760 mm.   **Voltage:** 6.6 kV ac 25 Hz.
One Hour Rating: 420 kW.   **Weight in Full Working Order:** 49.8 tonnes.
Maximum Tractive Effort: 102 kN.   **Length over Buffers:** 11.020 m.
Driving Wheel Dia.: 800 mm.   **Max. Speed:** 50 km/h.

1099 001-8 **M**	SP	1099 006-7 **M**	SP	1099 011-7 **M**	SP
1099 002-6 **M**	SP	1099 007-5 **M**	SP	1099 012-5 **M**	SP
1099 003-4 **M**	SP	1099 008-3 **M**	SP	1099 013-3 **M**	SP
1099 004-2 **M**	SP	1099 009-1 **M**	SP	1099 014-1 **M**	SP
1099 005-9 **M**	SP	1099 010-9 **M**	SP	1099 016-6 **M**	SP

DIESEL LOCOMOTIVES

CLASS 2090   Bo

This small locomotive shunts at Waidhofen a.d. Ybbs.

Built: 1930.   **Engine:** Saurer BXD Petrol.
Builder: Floridsdorf.   **Power:** 88 kW (118 hp).
Gauge: 760 mm.   **Transmission:** Electric.
Maximum Tractive Effort: 20 kN.   **Weight in Full Working Order:** 12 tonnes.
Driving Wheel Dia.: 800 mm.   **Length over Buffers:** 5.62 m.
Max. Speed: 40 km/h.

2090 001-5	WH	

CLASS 2190   MARIAZELL BAHN   Bo

This locomotive is used as the works shunter at HW St. Pölten. The class once totalled three, the other two now being preserved.

59

Built: 1934.
Builder – Mech.Parts: Simmering.
Gauge: 760 mm.
Maximum Tractive Effort: 22 kN.
Driving Wheel Dia.: 800 mm.
Max. Speed: 45 km/h.

Engine: Simmering SV8.
Power: 86 kW (115 hp).
Transmission: Electric.
Weight in Full Working Order: 12 tonnes.
Length over Buffers: 5.72 m.

2190 003-0   SP

CLASS 2091   MARIAZELLBAHN   1–Bo–1

These locomotives can be found on three of the narrow gauge systems working light passenger trains.

Built: 1936–40.
Builder: Simmering.
Gauge: 760 mm.
Maximum Tractive Effort: 34 kN.
Driving Wheel Dia.: 820 mm.
Max. Speed: 50 km/h.

Engine: Simmering R8.
Power: 155 kW (208 hp).
Transmission: Electric. Siemens.
Weight in Full Working Order: 23.2 tonnes.
Length over Buffers: 10.80 m.

2091 001-4   SP   2091 003-0   SP   2091 005-5   SP
2091 002-2 **N**   GM

CLASS 2092   MARIAZELL BAHN   C

These are used on pilot duties on their respective systems. They are in fact Wehrmacht type HF 130 C locomotives rebuilt with larger cabs and other detail alterations.

Built: 1943–44.
Builder: Gmeinder/Windhoff.
Gauge: 760 mm.
Maximum Tractive Effort: 49 kN.
Driving Wheel Dia.: 700 mm.
Max. Speed: 25 km/h.

Engine: Deutz 6 M517.
Power: 100 kW (134hp).
Transmission: Hydraulic.
Weight in Full Working Order: 16.5 tonnes.
Length over Buffers: 5.325 m.

The unique 2093 01, repainted in original green livery, on display at St. Pölten Alpenbahnhot on 18/09/87.   *Brian Garvin*

2092 001-3　　SP　　　　2092 003-9　　SP　　　2092 004-7　　GM
2092 002-1　　ZS

CLASS 2093　　　　　　　　　　　　　　　　　　Bo–Bo

This unique locomotive sees sporadic use shunting at St. Pölten Alpenbahnhof, and on works trains on the Mariazell line. It was repainted green for the 1987 celebrations.

Built: 1930.　　　　　　　　　　　**Engine:** SGP R8.
Builder: Graz.　　　　　　　　　　**Power:** 150 kW (201 hp).
Gauge: 760 mm.　　　　　　　　　 **Transmission:** Electric. Siemens.
Maximum Tractive Effort: 42 kN.　**Weight in Full Working Order:** 34 tonnes.
Driving Wheel Dia.: 850 mm.　　　**Length over Buffers:** 9.65 m.
Max. Speed: 35 km/h.

2093 001-2 **G**　　SP

CLASS 2095　　　　　　　　　　　　　　　　　　　B–B

The standard ÖBB locomotive for the narrow gauge which is found on all existing lines. The SP locos rarely work on the electrified line to Mariazell except in emergencies.

Built: 1958–62.　　　　　　　　　　**Engine:** SGP S12a.
Builders: SGP Floridsdorf.　　　　**Power:** 440 kW (590 hp).
Gauge: 760 mm.　　　　　　　　　 **Transmission:** Hydraulic.
Maximum Tractive Effort: 98 kN.　**Weight in Full Working Order:** 30 tonnes.
Driving Wheel Dia.: 900 mm.　　　**Length over Buffers:** 10.40 m.
Max. Speed: 60 km/h.

2095 001-0	ZS	2095 006-9 **N**	SP	2095 011-9 **N**	SP
2095 002-8	ZS	2095 007-7	GM	2095 012-7	GM
2095 003-6	ZS	2095 008-5 **N**	WH	2095 013-5	SP
2095 004-4	SP	2095 009-3	WH	2095 014-3	GM
2095 005-1	WH	2095 010-1 **N**	WH	2095 015-0 **N**	SP

DIESEL RAILCARS

CLASS 5090　　　　　　　　　　　　　　　　　　B–B

The ZS units are used on the Krimml line whilst the GM units are used on the Gmünd–Gross Gerungs line. Two more are on order for delivery 2–3/90.

Built: 1986.
Builder: Knotz.
Gauge: 760 mm.
Engine:
Transmission: Electric.
Multiple Working: Up to four cars can work in multiple.
Seats: 64S.　　　　　　　　　　　**Length over Couplings:** 18.30 m.
Weight: 29 tonnes.　　　　　　　 **Max. Speed:** 70 km/h.

5090 001-8 **R**	ZS	5090 004-2 **R**	GM	5090 006-7 **R**
5090 002-6 **R**	ZS	5090 005-9 **R**	GM	5090 007-5 **R**
5090 003-4 **R**	ZS			

CLASS 5099　　　　　　　　　　　　RACK RAILCARS(2–B)

These work exclusively on the Schafbergbahn.

Built: 1964.　　　　　　　　　　　**Transmission:** Hydraulic.
Builder: SGP.　　　　　　　　　　**Seats:** 78S.
Gauge: 1000 mm.　　　　　　　　 **Weight:** 32.9 tonnes.
Engine: SGP S8 of 330 kW.　　　 **Length over Couplings:** 14.89 m.
Max. Speed: 12 km/h (rack), 20 km/h (adhesion).

5099 001-9　　SW　　　　5099 002-7　　SW

▲The standard modern narrow-gauge diesel-hydraulic class is the 2095. 2095 002-8 is seen at Zell-am-See on 01/08/86. *John Stein*

▼Rack railcar 5099 002-7 is seen at St. Wolfgang on 30/09/87. *Brian Garvin*

DEPARTMENTAL STOCK

SMALL SHUNTERS ('KLEINLOKS')

The original system of numbering was based on that of the DRG as follows:

K	Kleinlok.
b	benzol (petrol).
ö	öl (diesel).
g	gas (Holzgasgenerator).
e	electric transmission.
f	flüssigkeitsbetrieb (hydraulic transmission).
s	speicher fahrzeug (storage vehicle, i.e. battery).

A new system was adopted on 1st January 1957 when the classification number absorbed all the above details.

The first digit (1) means kleinlok.

The second digit refers to the traction system as follows:

1	diesel mechanical
3	diesel electric
5	diesel hydraulic
7	battery electric.

The third digit is for different types or builders.

All were prefixed by 'X' denoting departmental stock. The new computer numbering system replaces the 'X' with a zero, but some locos still retain the former number.

Computer Number	1957 No.	DRG System		Location	Type	Power (kW)
0111 005-8	(X 111.05)	Kb	5160	Oberbaustofflager Zeltweg	B dm	46
0111 007-1	(X 111.07)	Kb	5162	SP ✒	B dm	46
0112 003-5	(X 112.03)	Kg	4688	WE	B dm	76
0112 006-8	(X 112.06)	Kö	4801	Bahnmeisterei Meidling	B dm	76
0112 007-6	(X 112.07)	Kg	4811	KD	B dm	76
0130 002-1	(X 130.02)	Köe	4085	WL (Saalfelden)	Bo de	76
0130 003-9	(X 130.03)	Köe	4922	WL	Bo de	76
0150 001-1	(X 150.01)	Kbf	5104	WN	B dh	80
0150 002-9	(X 150.02)	Kbf	5105	LZ	B dh	80
0150 003-7	(X 150.03)	Kbf	5108	KD (Vordernberg)	B dh	80
0150 004-5	(X 150.04)	Kbf	5110	WN	B dh	80
0150 005-2	(X 150.05)	Kbf	5111	LZ	B dh	80
0150 008-6	(X 150.08)	Kbf	5114	Fürnitz (Bauleitung)	B dh	80
0150 009-4	(X 150.09)	Kbf		LZ	B dh	80
0170 001-2	(X 170.01)	Ks	4866	HW Floridsdorf	Bo ae	80
0170 002-0	(X 170.02)	Ks	4818	HW Floridsdorf	Bo ae	80

HEATING UNITS

These are former locos used as stationary heating units. They cannot be used for traction except where shown below. Those shown as being in full working order double as working preserved locos, and are also shown in the 'Preserved locomotives' list.

Number	Formerly	Location
01101	1073.08	Wels Vbf
01102	1280.10	MZ
01103	1280.18	WN
01104	1089.05	Linz Hbf
01106	4041.03	HW Floridsdorf (Restored as ET 10 03 in full working order)
01107	4041.05	HW Floridsdorf
01108	1280.17	Bad Ischl
01109	1073.17	Hohenau
01110	1073.20	Salzburg Gnigl
01111	1073.16	Kufstein
01113	1280.16	Röhr

▲Departmental shunter X 150.03 is seen at HW St. Pölten during 1986. Not all of this class have been renumbered. ÖBB

▼Plasser TASC vehicle X 627.055 is seen in the Strasshof parade of 13/09/87. *Peter Fox*

01115	1670.01	Villach West
01116	1670.20	Feldkirch
01117	1670.21	HW SP
01118	1670.25	Zfl Floridsdorf (In full working order)
01119	1670.02	Salzburg (Hbf sub-shed)
01120	1670.102	Linz
01121	1670.06	Sigmundsherberg
01122	1670.26	Wiener Neustadt
01123	1670.28	Salzburg (Hbf sub-shed)
01124	1670.14	Amstetten
01125	1670.09	Innsbruck (In full working order)
01126	1670.104	Bludenz (In full working order)
01127	1020.47	HW Floridsdorf (In full working order)
01128	1145.09	HW Floridsdorf
01129	1018.05	LZ (In full working order)
	1670.27	HW Knittelfeld

AWS TEST UNIT ('INDUSIMESSWAGEN')

Only one has been reported and it can pop up anywhere on the ÖBB system. Max Speed 50/80 km/h.

X 431.01   Knotz 10400/11456 of 1972.

SELF-PROPELLLED OVERHEAD LINE INSPECTION UNITS ('MOTORTURMWAGEN')

These are overhead line maintenance units belonging to the electrical department and are allocated to various places for repairs or maintenance to the catenary. These depots can be found at sub-stations or in specially constructed sheds near stations and yards. A common feature of all these units is the lifting platform found on top of the unit which can be adjusted in height or even revolved so that it sticks out over adjoining lines.

X 512   1–A

No technical details available.

X 512.03   Sigmundsherberg | X 512.06   Villach

X 532   1–A

Built: 1953–60.
Builder – Mech Parts: Franz Knotz, Tobisch.
Engine: JW 100   **Transmission:** Electric.
Power: 76 kW (102 hp)   **Weight in Full Working Order:** 19.6 tonnes.
Driving Wheel Dia.: 900 mm.   **Length over Buffers:** 7.86 m.
Max. Speed: 80 km/h.

X 532.26	Reutte in Tirol	X 532.53	Villach
X 532.41	Simmering	X 532.54	Linz-Kleinmünchen
X 532.42	Wiener Neustadt	X 532.55	St. Michael
X 532.43	Wolfurt	X 532.56	Gänserndorf
X 532.44	Feldkirch	X 532.57	Golling-Abtenau
X 532.45	Linz-Kleinmünchen	X 532.58	Penzing
X 532.46	Salzburg	X 532.59	Selzthal
X 532.47	Villach	X 532.60	Amstetten
X 532.48	Penzing	X 532.61	Graz
X 532.49	VIllach	X 532.62	Attnang Puchheim
X 532.50	Hall in Tirol	X 532.63	Bruck a. d. Leitha
X 532.51	Penzing	X 532.64	Salzburg
X 532.52	Penzing	X 532.65	Hütteldorf

X 532.S (760 mm gauge) MARIA ZELLBAHN

Built: 1964.
Builder – Mech Parts: Franz Knotz, Tobisch.
Engine: JW 100
Power: 76 kW (102 hp)
Driving Wheel Dia.: 940 mm.
Max. Speed: 45 km/h.
Transmission: Electric.
Weight in Full Working Order: 15 tonnes.
Length over Buffers: 7.86 m.

X 532.S.01 St. Pölten   X 532.S.02 St. Pölten

X 533   1–A

No technical details available.

X 533.32	Innsbruck	X 533.34	Villach
X 533.33	Linz-Kleinmünchen	X 533.35	Penzing

X 534   1–A

Built: 1963–78 (1970–83*).
Engine: JW 200 (MAN D2566MTE*)
Power: 94 kW.
Weight: 20.5 tonnes.
Maximum Speed: 80 km/h.
Transmission: Electric (Brown-Boveri).
Wheel Diameter: 940 tonnes.
Length over Buffers: 7.74 m.

X 534.01	Innsbruck	X 534.44		Attnang Puchheim
X 534.02	Bad Ausee	X 534.45		Innsbruck
X 534.03	Innsbruck	X 534.47		Simmering
X 534.05	Saalfelden	X 534.48		Floridsdorf
X 534.06	Villach	X 534.49		Villach
X 534.07	Villach	X 534.50		Villach
X 534.08	Wiener Neustadt	X 534.51		Bruck a. d. Leitha
X 534.09	Landeck	X 534.52		Brigittenau
X 534.10	Innsbruck	X 534.53		Wolfurt
X 534.11	Innsbruck	X 534.54		Landeck
X 534.12	Innsbruck	X 534.55		Pregarten
X 534.13	Reutte in Tirol	X 534.56		Tulln
X 534.14	Marihof-St. Lambrecht	X 534.57		St. Anton am Arlberg
X 534.15	St. Michael	X 534.58		Hütteldorf
X 534.16	Schladming	X 534.59		Dorfgastein
X 534.17	Hütteldorf	X 534.60		Salzburg
X 534.18	Ebensee	X 534.61		Wartberg a. d. Krems
X 534.19	Floridsdorf	X 534.62		Gänserndorf
X 534.20	Stockerau	X 534.63		Matrei
X 534.21	Selzthal	X 534.64		Floridsdorf
X 534.22	Warmbad Villach	X 534.65		Mallnitz
X 534.23	Wörgl	X 534.66		Linz Kleinmünchen
X 534.24	Steindorf bei Strasswalchen	X 534.67		Wiener Neustadt
X 534.25	Simmering	X 534.68		Brigittenau
X 534.26	Klein Reifling	X 534.69		Tulln
X 534.27	Amstetten	X 534.70	*	Amstetten
X 534.28	Feldkirch	X 534.71	*	Semmering
X 534.30	Hieflau	X 534.72	*	St. Johann in Pongau
X 534.31	Penzing	X 534.73	*	Salzburg
X 534.32	Innsbruck	X 534.74	*	Semmering
X 534.34	St. Veit a. d. Glan	X 534.75	*	Kitzbühel
X 534.35	Riedau	X 534.76	*	Bruck a. d. Mur
X 534.36	St. Pölten	X 534.77	*	Saalfelden
X 534.37	Knittelfeld	X 534.78	*	Meidling
X 534.38	Linz-Kleinmünchen	X 534.79	*	St. Pölten —
X 534.39	Graz	X 534.80	*	Villach
X 534.40	Salzburg	X 534.81	*	Meidling
X 534.41	Wald am Arlberg	X 534.82	*	Meidling
X 534.42	Penzing	X 534.83	*	Warmbad Villach
X 534.43	Golling-Abtenau			

X 535   Bo

Fitted with a hydraulic lifting platform and a pantograph. The first two are being evaluated before placing orders for a production run.

Built: 1983.   **Transmission:** Electric.
Builder – Mechanical Parts: Franz Knotz.   **Wheel Diameter:** 1000 mm.
Builder – Electrical Parts: Brown Boveri.   **Length over Buffers:** 13.06 m.
Engine: MAN D 2542 MLE (12 cyl.)   **Power:** 363 kW at 2100 rpm.
Max. Speed: 100 km/h (own power). 120 km/h (hauled).
Disc & Rheostatic braking.

X 535.01   Hall-in-Tirol |X 535.02   Simmering

X 551   B–2

Fitted with a hydraulic platform, pantograph, and a trench digging arm.

Built: 1983.   **Transmission:** Hydraulic.
Builder: Plasser & Theurer.   **Wheel Diameter:** 710 mm.
Engine: Deutz KHD BF 12L 413 FC.   **Length over Buffers:** 15.34 m.
Power: 349 kW at 2500 rpm.   **Weight:** 45 tonnes.
Max. Speed.: 100 km/h (own power). 120 km/h (hauled).

X 551.01   Linz Kleinmünchen

PW TROLLEYS (MOTOR BAHN WAGEN MBW)

These are usually purely staff transporters and are numbered X625.01 onwards with a separate series in the 900s for narrow gauge vehicles. No details of individual vehicles available.

TRACK MACHINES (OBERBAUWAGEN OBW)

This is the largest group of departmentals after the X 500 series o.l.e. units. They appear in many guises having various attachments to the main frame such as rotary snow ploughs, ordinary snow ploughs and are also used as ballast spreaders, hydraulic grabs, cranes, etc. They have normal buffing and coupling gear and can be used to haul wagons to engineering sites. Information is incomplete and details of observations welcomed. All built by Plasser.

No.	Works Build No.	Date	Base	Fittings,notes,etc.
X 627.001	14	1974	Streckenleitung WF	Crane, grab arm, ballast plough.
X 627.011	456	1980	Streckenleitung WN	Crane, ballast plough.
X 627.021	457	1981	Bauleitung Wien	Crane, ballast plough.
X 627.022	469	1982	Streckenleitung WN	Crane, ballast plough.
X 627.023	470	1982	Streckenleitung Leoben	Crane, ballast plough.
X 627.031	480	1983	Streckenleitung VH Baumeister Rosenbach.	Crane, ballast plough, sleeper grab.
X 627.032	481	1983	Strltg. Wien Sud Ost Baumeister WO.	Crane, ballast plough, sleeper grab.
X 627.033	483	1984	Streckenleitung GZ	Crane, ballast plough, sleeper grab. Classed OBW–105, 27 tonnes, 100 km/h.
X 627.034	484	1984	Streckenleitung SL	Crane, ballast plough, sleeper grab.
X 627.035	487	1984	Streckenleitung BL, Wolfurt	
X 627.036	488	1984	Strltg NS, Semmering	Tunnel emergency vehicle.
X 627.051	501	1985	Streckenleitung IN Bm IN.	Crane, sleeper grab.
X 627.052	502	1985	Streckenleitung LZ Bm LZ.	Crane, sleeper grab.
X 627.053	503	1985	Streckenleitung LZ Bm WE.	Crane, sleeper grab, ballast plough.
X 627.054	504	1985	Streckenleitung WF.	Crane, sleeper grab, ballast plough.
X 627.055	516	1987	Streckenleitung WF.	Crane, sleeper grab, ballast plough.
X 627.101	15	1975	Linz Wegscheid	No crane, used for shunting.
X 627.501	454	1978	Streckenleitung VH	Crane, rotary snowplough.
X 627.511	479	1984	Strltg Wien Sud Ost Vbf Kledering	Crane, ballast plough, sleeper grab, Rotary snowplough, other winter fittings.
X 627.512	485	1984	Strltg. VH, Arnoldstein.	Crane, sleeper grab, winter fittings.
X 627.513	518	1987	Strltg. VH, Arnoldstein.	Crane, sleeper grab, winter fittings.
X 627.514	519	1987	Strltg. Spittal/M. BM Spittal.	Crane, sleeper grab, winter fittings.
X 627.701	517	1987	Bahnmeister WW	Grab arm, tunnel emergency vehicle.

X 627.801   Track test unit.
X 627.951 513 1986 Mariazellerbahn   Multi-purpose vehicle.

Looking very smart in white and red livery is this 1983 built overhead line unit X 535.02, seen in the Strasshof parade.   *Peter Fox*

SNOWPLOUGHS

The snowploughs detailed here have been generally built on the frames of old locomotives. Standard gauge snowploughs have been renumbered in the UIC wagon series.

Narrow Gauge:

Number	Formerly	
985.03		WH
985.05		GM
985.06		GM
985.50	299.02	ZS
986.10		PB
986.20		GM

Standard Gauge:

New Number	Old Number	Formerly	
80 81 9760 150-9	985.111		WO
80 81 9760 200-2	985.120	30.104	AM
80 81 9760 201-0	985.124	360.12	GZ
80 81 9760 202-8	985.127	360.18	SP
80 81 9760 300-0	985.200	52.765	WE

```
80 81 9760 301-8    985.201    52.458     VH
80 81 9760 302-6    985.202    52.1448    Bruck a.d. Leitha
80 81 9760 303-4    985.203    52.357     BO
80 81 9760 304-2    985.204    52.401     SB
80 81 9760 305-9    985.205    52.1239    SL
80 81 9760 306-7    985.206    52.2397    VH
80 81 9760 307-5    985.207    52.433     LE
80 81 9760 308-3    985.208    52.1722    AT
80 81 9760 309-1    985.209    52.3602    KN
80 81 9760 310-9    985.210    52.1594    LE
80 81 9760 311-7    985.211    52.6649    BL
80 81 9760 312-5    985.212    52.4943    GZ
80 81 9760 313-3    985.213    52.6940    Hieflau
80 81 9760 314-1    985.214    52.3636    VH
80 81 9760 315-9    985.215    52.3941    MZ
80 81 9760 316-6    985.216    52.3174    Saalfelden
80 81 9760 317-4    985.217    52.1719    MZ
80 81 9760 318-2    985.218    52.6765    WL
80 81 9760 319-0    985.219    52.6969    BO
80 81 9760 320-8    985.220    52.7052    KD
80 81 9760 321-6    985.221    52.7295    WO
80 81 9760 322-4    985.222    52.3553    LZ
80 81 9760 323-2    985.223    52.6312    VD
80 81 9760 324-0    985.224    52.478     WN
80 81 9760 325-7    985.225    52.3615    NS
80 81 9760 326-5    985.226    52.3520    Mistelbach
80 81 9760 327-3    985.227    52.2374    WN
80 81 9760 328-1    985.228    52.7213    GM
80 81 9760 329-9    985.229    52.2428    BL
80 81 9760 330-7    985.230    52.7100    IN
80 81 9760 331-5    985.231    52.7595    IN
80 81 9760 032-9               52.1442    BL
80 81 9760 033-7               52.7053    WO (Kledering Yard)
```

BREAKDOWN CRANES

New Date	Old	Depot	Carry	Builder
80 81 9766 040-6	966.400	KD	45 tonnes	Kunz, Bodensee 1980
80 81 9766 041-4	966.401	KD	45 tonnes	Gyor 1945
80 81 9766 042-2	966.402	IN	45 tonnes	Gyor 1945
80 81 9766 050-5	966.500	WO	80 tonnes	Kirow, Leipzig 1967
80 81 9766 051-3	966.501	WO	80 tonnes	Kirow, Leipzig 1967
80 81 9766 066-4	966.600	WE	125 tonnes	Kirow, Leipzig 1975

SHIPS & BOATS

Bodensee (Lake Constance)

Vessel	Builder	Date	Displacement (empty)	Pass.	Power
MS Austria	Korneuburg	1939	352 tonnes	1200	1270 kW
MB Dornbirn	Korneuburg	1956	40 tonnes	100	300 kW
MB Feldkirch	Korneuburg	1955	40 tonnes	100	300 kW
MB Montafon	Korneuburg	1957	42 tonnes	160	300 kW
MS Österreich	Korneuburg	1928	281 tonnes	600	1200 kW
MS Vorarlberg	Korneuburg	1964	392 tonnes	1000	1200 kW

Wolfgangsee

Vessel	Builder	Date	Displacement (empty)	Pass.	Power
MS Elisabeth		1873		270	135 kW
MS Falkenstein		1959		270	150 kW
MS Kaiser Franz Josef		1872		225	115 kW
MS Österreich		1984		365	173 kW
MS Salzkammergut		1973		300	170 kW
MB St. Wolfgang		1950		80	115 kW

INDEPENDENT RAILWAYS

STATUS CODES

Austria still has many private railways offering feeder services into the ÖBB network or simply providing local transport often in quite delightful backwaters. Most of these lines have retained the old style classifications which have a prefix letter to explain the type of traction:

E   (Elektrolokomotive)   Electric locomotive.
ET   (Elektrotriebewagen)   Electric railcar.
V   (Verbrennungsmotoren)   Diesel locomotive.
VT   (Verbrennungstriebwagen)   Diesel railcar.
X   Departmental.

On the Steiermarkische Landesbahnen some additional classifications exist whilst the GySEV uses the MÁV (Hungarian State Railways) classification. Lines are standard gauge except where otherwise shown.

ACHENSEEBAHN   AB

Gauge: 1000 mm.
Depot: Jenbach.
Timetable: 31a.

This line is only open in the summer months and features Riggenbach rack and adhesion working as the locos propel their trains on the rack from Jenbach to Eben and then run round to haul their trains to the terminus.

Number	Wheels	Built	km/h	NAME or notes
1	0–4–0RT	1899	20	Eben am Achensee
2	0–4–0RT	1899	20	Jenbach
3	0–4–0RT	1899	20	Achenkirch

GRAZ KÖFLACHER BAHN   GKB

Depots: Graz GKB (Main Depot/Works). Wies Eibiswald, Köflach (Subsheds).

This line celebrated its 125th Anniversary early in 1985. Its main traffic is coal but in recent years the passenger services have become just as important and new rolling stock is still in course of delivery. The steam locomotives have no booked workings having been retained for excursion use.

Number	Wheels	Built	kW	km/h	NAME or notes
671	0–6–0	1860	284	45	
56.3115	2–8–0	1914	787	60	
50.1171	2–10–0	1942	1200	80	
V 80.1	B dh	1938	60		Köf type.
V 100.1	A1 dm	1978	76	25	Homebuilt tractor using parts of tampers.
V 100.2	A1 dm	1980	76	25	Homebuilt tractor using parts of tampers.
V 360.1	C dh	1943	265	60	Formerly ÖBB 2065.01.
V 390.1	C dh	1955	294	60	
V 600.1	C dh	1973	441	60	
V 600.2	C dh	1973	441	60	
V 600.3	C dh	1973	441	60	
V 700.1	C dh	1977	515	48	
V 750.1	C de	1964	550	60	MW fitted
V 750.2	Co de	1965	550	60	MW fitted
V 750.3	Co de	1969	550	60	MW fitted
V 1500.1	BB dh	1975	1100	100	no train heating.
V 1500.2	BB dh	1975	1100	100	no train heating.
V 1500.3	BB dh	1975	1100	100	no train heating.
V 1500.4	BB dh	1975	1100	100	no train heating.
V 1500.5	BB dh	1977	1100	100	no train heating.
V 1500.6	BB dh	1978	1100	100	no train heating.
VT 10.01	AA dm	1953	220	90	

```
VT 10.02   AA dm      1953  220   90
VT 10.03   AA dm      1955  220   90
VT 10.05   AA dm      1955  220   90
VT 10.06   AA dm      1956  220   90
VT 10.07   AA dm      1958  220   90
VT 10.08   AA dm      1962  220   90
VT 10.09   AA dm      1968  220   90
VT 50.01   A1 dm      1952  110   90   Formerly DB 795 169.
VT 50.04   A1 dm      1952  110   90   Formerly DB 795 255.
VT 70.01   Bo–2–Bo de 1980  250   90   Articulated 2 car DMU.
VT 70.02   Bo–2–Bo de 1980  250   90
VT 70.03   Bo–2–Bo de 1980  250   90
VT 70.04   Bo–2–Bo de 1981  250   90
VT 70.05   Bo–2–Bo de 1981  250   90
VT 70.06   Bo–2–Bo de 1985  250   90
VT 70.07   Bo–2–Bo de 1985  250   90
VT 70.08   Bo–2–Bo de 1985  250   90
VT 70.09   Bo–2–Bo de 1985  250   90
VT 70.10   Bo–2–Bo de 1985  250   90
VT 70.11   Bo–2–Bo de 1985  250   90
VT 70.12   Bo–2–Bo de 1985  250   90
VT 70.13   Bo–2–Bo de 1985  250   90
```

GYÖR–SOPRON–EBENFURTI VASÚT   GySEV

Depots: Sopron (Main Depot/Works). Fertöszentmiklos, Györ (Subsheds).
Timetable: 52g, 73a.

This is an international railway jointly owned by Austria and Hungary – a survivor of the old empire! It uses the Hungarian style of classification.

Number	Wheels	Built	kW	km/h	NAME or notes
17	0–6–0	1885	206	55	
124	2–6–2T	1950	243	60	MÁV 375 type.
424.064	4–8–0	1941	993	90	Ex MÁV.
M43.2501	BB dh	1980	331	60	CFR 86 MÁV M43.
M43.2502	BB dh	1980	331	60	CFR 86 MÁV M43.
M43.2503	BB dh	1980	331	60	CFR 86 MÁV M43.
M44.301	Bo–Bo de	1957	450	80	Same as MÁV M44 ex MÁV M44.001.
M44.302	Bo–Bo de	1959	450	80	Same as MÁV M44 ex MÁV M44.025.
M44.303	Bo–Bo de	1969	450	80	Same as MÁV M44.
M44.304	Bo–Bo de	1969	450	80	Same as MÁV M44.
M44.305	Bo–Bo de	1970	450	80	Same as MÁV M44.
M44.306	Bo–Bo de	1971	450	80	Same as MÁV M44.
M44.307	Bo–Bo de	1971	450	80	Same as MÁV M44.
M47.1501	BB dh	1975	552	70	CFR 85 MÁV M47.
M47.1502	BB dh	1975	552	70	CFR 85 MÁV M47.
M62.901	Co–Co de	1972	1500	100	Same as MÁV M62.
M62.902	Co–Co de	1972	1500	100	Same as MÁV M62.
M62.903	Co–Co de	1972	1500	100	Same as MÁV M62.
M62.904	Co–Co de	1972	1500	100	Same as MÁV M62.
M62.905	Co–Co de	1972	1500	100	Same as MÁV M62.
M62.907	Co–Co de	1971	1500	100	Formerly MÁV M62.142.
M62.908	Co–Co de	1971	1500	100	Formerly MÁV M62.143.
V43.320	Bo–Bo e	1984	2220	130	Formerly MÁV V43.1320.
V43.321	Bo–Bo e	1984	2220	130	Formerly MÁV V43.1321.
V43.322	Bo–Bo e	1984	2220	130	Formerly MÁV V43.1322.
V43.323	Bo–Bo e	1984	2220	130	Formerly MÁV V43.1323.
V43.324	Bo–Bo e	1984	2220	130	Formerly MÁV V43.1324.
V43.325	Bo–Bo e	1984	2220	130	Formerly MÁV V43.1325.
V43.326	Bo–Bo e	1984	2220	130	Formerly MÁV V43.1326.
V43.327	Bo–Bo e	1984	2220	130	Formerly MÁV V43.1327.
V43.328	Bo–Bo e	1984	2220	130	Formerly MÁV V43.1328.
V43.329	Bo–Bo e	1984	2220	130	Formerly MÁV V43.1329.
V43.330	Bo–Bo e	1984	2220	130	Formerly MÁV V43.1330.

Achenseebahn No. 1 'Eben am Achensee' arrives at Achensee on 17/08/87 with 15.25 from Jenbach, the locomotive hauling the train from Eben after pushing its coaches up the rack section.

David C. Rodgers

▲**GKB.** Diesel railcars VT 70.02 and VT 70.09 are seen at Graz GKB shed on 21/08/86.

Brian Garvin

▼**SVB.** ET 45 'Lamprechtshausen' on the 13.20 Lamprechtshausen–Salzburg at Bürmoos.

Peter Fox

V43.331	Bo–Bo e	1984	2220	130	Formerly MÁV V43.1331.
VF 100					Heating unit. Sopron station. Ex MÁV V42 529.
ABbmot 1	A1A–2 dm	1956	335	100	DMU.
ABbmot 2	A1A–2 dm	1956	335	100	DMU.
Bzmot 501	1–A dh	1981	130	70	DMU (as CSD M152).
Bzmot 502	1–A dh	1981	130	70	DMU (as CSD M152).
Bamot 701	1AA1 dh	1962	220	90	DMU.
Bamot 702	1AA1 dh	1962	220	90	DMU.

MONTAFONERBAHN AG   MBS

Depot: Schruns.
Timetable: 42.

This 12.8 km line runs from the ÖBB junction to Bludenz to a terminal at Schruns – hence the abbreviation MBS.

Number	Wheels	Built	kW	km/h	NAME or notes
1045.01	Bo–Bo	1927	1140	60	Ex ÖBB.
1045.03	Bo–Bo	1927	1140	60	Ex ÖBB.
ET 10.101	1A–A1	1950	185	75	
ET 10.103	Bo–Bo	1935	370	100	Rebuilt DB VT 63 905 (1965).
ET 10.104	Bo–Bo	1935	370	100	Rebuilt DB VT 63 907 (1974).
4130.02	Bo–Bo EMU	1958	1260	130	Ex ÖBB.
7130.01	trailer	1958		130	Ex ÖBB.
6130.02	trailer	1958		130	Ex ÖBB.
V 10.016	D dh	1956	590	64	Ex Köln Bonner Eisenbahn.
V 10.021	Bo de	1927	130	50	
VT 10.111	A1 dm	1955	110	90	
XVT 10.903	AA dm	1965	220	90	Rebuilt ÖBB 5081.12.

SALZBURGER STADTWERKE VERKEHRSBETRIEBE   SVB

Depot/Works: Salzburg Itzling.
Timetable: 21.

This line runs from outside the ÖBB station in Salzburg to Lamprechtshausen (25 km). Electrified at 1000 V dc.

Number	Wheels	Built	kW	km/h	NAME or notes
E 11	Bo	1913	150	30	
E 61	Bo–Bo	1952	380	60	
E 62	Bo–Bo	1952	380	60	
E 63	Bo–Bo	1952	264	50	Ex SAKOG E 27.002.
E 71	Bo–Bo	1986	600	60	
ET 1	Bo	1919	126	40	Departmental.
ET 2	Bo	1911	126	40	Departmental. Rail welding car.
ET 3	Bo	1908	126	40	Departmental.
ET 4	Bo	1908	126	40	Departmental.
ET 5	Bo	1908	126	40	
ET 6	Bo	1908	306	60	
ET 7	Bo	1907	306	60	
ET 23	Bo–Bo	1964	400	80	Ex Köln Bonner Eisenbahn ET 203.
ET 24	Bo–Bo	1964	400	80	Ex Köln Bonner Eisenbahn ET 204.
ET 31	Bo–Bo	1952	380	60	
ET 32	Bo–Bo	1952	380	60	
ET 33	Bo–Bo	1951	612	60	
ET 41	Bo–2–Bo	1983	600		Stadt Salzburg
ET 42	Bo–2–Bo	1983	600		Bergheim
ET 43	Bo–2–Bo	1983	600		Oberndorf
ET 44	Bo–2–Bo	1983	600		Bürmoos
ET 45	Bo–2–Bo	1983	600		Lamprechtshausen
ET 46	Bo–2–Bo	1983	600		Anthering
ET 47	Bo–2–Bo	1983	600		Nussdorf
ET 48	Bo–2–Bo	1983	600		Göming

ET 49	Bo–2–Bo	1983	600		St. Gorgen
ET 50	Bo–2–Bo	1983	600		Freilassing
B 105	2	1909			
B 108	2	1911			
B 116	2	1908			
B 301	2–2	1950		60	
B 302	2–2	1950		60	
B 303	2–2	1950		60	
B 304	2–2	1950		60	
B 305	2–2	1950		60	
B 306	2–2	1950		60	
X 91		1977			Plasser tamper. Type 1-77L.

STEIERMARKISCHE LANDESBAHNEN   StLB

The Austrian province of Steiermark has many standard and narrow gauge lines grouped together and run by the local government. There are some 47 km of standard gauge and 120 km of narrow gauge lines. Although managed by a central office, stock rarely changes from one line to another.

Feldbach–Bad Gleichenberg. (21.2 km. Electrified at 1000 V dc).

Depot: Feldbach.
Timetable: 52b.

Number	Wheels	Built	kW	km/h	NAME or notes
E 41	Bo–Bo	1930	400	50.	
ET 1	Bo–Bo	1930	295	50.	
ET 2	Bo–Bo	1930	295	50	Stored.
RT 1	B dm	1963	15		
X 51					

Gleisdorf–Weiz (14.7 km.).

Depot: Weiz.
Timetable: 52c.

DE 1	Co de	1964	550	60	
DE 2	Co de	1964	550	60	
VT 21	AA dm	1956	220	90	(Formerly DB 798 577)
VT 22	AA dm	1955	220	90	(Formerly DB 798 645)
VT 23	AA dm	1956	220	90	(Formerly DB 798 643)
VT 24	AA dm	1956	220	90	(Formerly ÖBB 5081 002)
VT 25	AA dm	1956	220	90	(Formerly ÖBB 5081 020)
X 41					

Peggau–Übelbach (10.25 km.).

Depot: Übelbach.
Timetable: 54.

ET 11	Bo–2	1936	400	100	(Formerly ÖBB 4042.01).
ET 12	Bo–2	1936	400	100	(Formerly ÖBB 4042.02).
ET 13	Bo–Bo	1949	1268	100	(Formerly Swiss SOB 62).
EB 21	2–2	1936		100	(Formerly ÖBB 6042.01).
EB 22	2–2	1955		100	(Formerly SBB coach).

Mixnitz–St. Erhard

A freight-only 10.4 km line. 760 mm gauge, electrified at 800 V dc but with its own standard gauge shunters for transfer work at the main-line junction.

Depot: Mixnitz.

VEL 1	Bo de	1956	48	18	Standard Gauge
VHL 2	B dh	1967	150	60	Standard Gauge
E 1	Bo	1913	122		760mm Gauge
E 2	Bo	1913	122		760mm Gauge
E 3	Bo–Bo	1957	150		760mm Gauge
E 4	Bo–Bo	1963	150		760mm Gauge

▲ Steiermarkische Landesbahn. VT 32 at Murau with 09.03 Unzmarkt–Tamsweg on 19/08/87.

David C. Rodgers

▼ Zillertalbahn. Four car diesel set VT4 stands at Jenbach on 08/09/85. *John Stein*

STERN UND HAFFERL

▲23.106 of the Gmunden–Vorchdorf line stands at Vorchdorf Eggenburg on 28/07/87.
Ian Futers

▼At Eferding on 01/10/87, ET 22.133 on a Linz–Peuerbach working passes E20.005 shunting.
Brian Garvin

Kapfenberg–Seebach

A freight-only 22.9 km line. 760 mm gauge.

VL11	Bo–Bo de	1964	260	50	
VL21	BB dh	1964	400	40	Formerly DB 251 901
VL22	BB dh	1972	485	50	Formerly JZ 740.023
VL23	BB dh	1972	485	50	Formerly JZ 740.024
X 43					
X 46					

Unzmarkt–Tamsweg

Known as the 'Murtalbahn', this 760 mm gauge line is 65.5 km long and used to go through to Mauterndorf.

Depot: Murau-Stozalpe (Main depot & works), Unzmarkt, Tamsweg (Sub-sheds).
Timetable: 63.

Bh 1	0–6–2T	1905	250	40	Formerly ÖBB 398.01
St 2	0–4–0T	1892		25	
U 40	0–6–2T	1908	160	45	
U 43	0–6–2T	1913	160	45	
VL 5	B dm	1938	60	25	
VL 6	B dh	1959	104	20	Formerly ZB D 11.
VL 7	C dh	1940	100	25	Wehrmacht HF 130 C type.
VL 12	Bo–Bo de	1966	389	50	EHRENFRIED
VL 13	Bo–Bo de	1967	389	50	FERDINAND
VL 16	Bo–Bo de	1967	315	50	ANTON
VT 31	Bo–Bo de	1980	221	70	Similar to ÖBB class 5090.
VT 32	Bo–Bo de	1981	221	70	Similar to ÖBB class 5090.
VT 33	Bo–Bo de	1981	221	70	Similar to ÖBB class 5090.
VT 34	Bo–Bo de	1981	221	70	Similar to ÖBB class 5090.
X 42					
X 45					
X 52					

Weiz–Birkfeld

Known as the 'Feistritztalbahn', this 760 mm gauge line is 24.1 km long and is nominally freight-only but with steam-hauled tourist trains in the summer.

Depot & Works: Weiz.
Timetable: 52c.

Kh 101	0–10–0T	1926	280	30	
U 44	0–6–2T	1922	160	45	
VL 4	C dh	1942	114	25	Wehrmacht HF 130 C type type.
VL 14	Bo–Bo de	1967	389	50	
VL 15	Bo–Bo de	1967	389	50	
RT 3	B dh	1957	41	25	
X 44					
X 53					

Wohlsdorf–Stainz

This 760 mm gauge line is closed to regular traffic but has been leased by the local community for tourist trains. 10.6 km long.

Depot: Stainz.

S 11	0–6–2T	1894	160	35	
U 8	0–6–2T	1894	160	45	
VL 3	C dh	1943	100	25	

STERN & HAFFERL   StH

This organisation runs several lines in Oberösterreich. Many of these lines use second-hand tramway equipment and offer a quaint way of travel through some backwater routes.

Details of the lines operated are as follows:

Burmoos–Trimmelkam. (BT)

An 8.8 km branch off the SVB, electrified at 1100 V dc.

Depot: Trimmelkam.
Timetable: 16a.

Gmunden–Vorchdorf.(GV)

A 14.6 km metre gauge line, electrified at 800 V dc.

Depot: Vorchdorf Eggenburg.
Timetable: 21.

Lambach–Haag.(LH)

A 26.3 km line, electrified at 800 V dc. As this line shares some tracks with the ÖBB which is electrified at 15 kV ac, two transformer vehicles are included in the fleet which are attached to trains before reaching ÖBB lines and detached on the return journey!

Depot: Haag.
Timetable: 16b.

Lambach–Vorchdorf.(LVE)

A 15.5 km standard gauge line.

Depot: Vorchdorf Eggenburg (shared with the narrow-gauge GV line).
Timetable: 16a.

Linz–Waizenkirchen (Linzer Lokalbahn) (LILO)

A 42.4 km suburban line out of Linz, electrified at 800 V dc. Some freight traffic.

Depots: Eferding, Waizenkirchen.
Timetable: 14c.

Neumarkt–Waizenkirchen–Peuerbach.(NWP)

This 16.5 km line now shares services with the LILO. Electrified at 800 V dc.

Depot: Peuerbach.
Timetable: 14c.

Vöcklamarkt–Attersee.(VA)

A 13.4 km metre gauge line electrified at 800 V dc.

The second digit of the numbering system denotes the owning company and the third digit denotes the type as follows:

Second digit:

20000	Stern und Hafferl		24000	LVE
21000	NWP		25000	LH
22000	LILO		26000	VA
23000	GV		27000	SAKOG

SAKOG is Salzach Kohlenbergbau Gesellschaft, i.e. Salzach Coal Company. This is situated at Trimmelkam at the end of the BT line.

Third digit:

This is 0 for a locomotive, 1 for a railcar and 2 for a trailer.

Note that vehicles are often, but not always, renumbered when transferred between lines. On renumbering, the last two digits are generally unaltered unless this would cause duplication. Renumberings shown are those which have occurred since the first edition of this book.

Number	Allocn.	Wheels	Built	kW	km/h	Notes
Locomotives.						
E 20.001	LH	Bo–Bo	1915	300	40	
E 20.004	LH	Bo–Bo	1916	200	40	
E 20.005	LILO	Bo–Bo	1915	200	40	
E 20.007	BT	Bo–Bo	1956	492	40	
E 20.008	LH	Bo–Bo	1941	300	60	Electro diesel. Former MBS E 10.002. Dumped.
E 20.010	LVE	Bo–Bo	1910	300	40	

ACTIVE ÖBB PRESERVED LOCOS

▲1670.25 (which doubles up as a heating unit) pulls a train of old four-wheeled stock at the Strasshof Parade on 13/09/87. *Peter Fox*

▼52.855 approaches to Wien Nord on 13/09/87 with a return excursion from Marchegg. *Peter Fox*

E 22.001	LILO	Bo–Bo	1915 200	40	
E 22.002	LILO	Bo	1912 80	25	
E 22.003	LILO	Bo–Bo	1916 316	50	
E 22.004	LILO	Bo–Bo	1912 600	40	Ex E 20.009.
E 27.001	BT	Bo–Bo	1952 292	50	

Dual voltage transformer units.

EGL 25.051LH	1A	1950 44	50
EGL 25.052LH	1A	1952 44	50

Standard Gauge Railcars.

ET 20.104	VA	Bo	1913 108	30	
ET 20.105	BT	Bo	1908 100	50	
ET 20.109	BT	Bo–Bo	1956 220	70	
ET 20.110	BT	Bo–Bo	1953 220	70	
ET 20.111	LVE	Bo–Bo	1953 320	70	
ET 21.103	LH	Bo	1912 108	50	Ex ET 22.103.
ET 21.104	LH	Bo	1912 158	50	Ex ET 22.104.
ET 21.105	LH	Bo	1921 108	50	Ex ET 22.105.
ET 21.106	NWP	Bo–Bo	1951 376	60	Ex ET 22.106, then ET 20.112.
ET 21.150	NWP	Bo	1908 108	50	
ET 22.101	LILO	Bo	1907 82	50	Ex ET 20.101.
ET 22.107	LILO	Bo–Bo	1951 376	60	
ET 22.130	LILO	Bo–Bo	1954 272	60	
ET 22.131	LILO	Bo–Bo	1954 272	60	
ET 22.132	LILO	Bo–Bo	1953 272	60	
ET 22.133	LILO	Bo–Bo	1953 272	60	
ET 22.134	LILO	Bo–Bo	1954 272	60	
ET 22.135	LILO	Bo–Bo	1953 272	60	
ET 22.136	LILO	Bo–Bo	1953 272	60	
ET 22.137	LILO	Bo–Bo	1954 272	60	
ET 22.141	LILO		1956	60	2-car unit ex KBE. Not yet in service.
ET 22.142	LILO		1956	60	2-car unit ex KBE. Not yet in service.
ET 22.143	LILO		1956	60	2-car unit ex KBE. Not yet in service.
ET 22.144	LILO		1956	60	2-car unit ex KBE. Not yet in service.
ET 24.101	LH	Bo	1931 106	50	
ET 24.102	LVE	Bo	1932 106	50	
ET 25.101	LH	Bo	1932 212	50	
ET 25.102	LH	Bo	1932 212	50	
ET 25.103	LH	Bo	1989 212		Dual voltage. Classified 4855 by the ÖBB.
ET 25.104	LH	Bo	1989 212		Dual voltage. Classified 4855 by the ÖBB.

Standard Gauge Trailers.

B 22.207	LILO	2–2	1950	
B 22.208	LILO	2–2	1950	
B 22.209	LILO	2–2	1950	
B 22.210	LILO	2–2	1950	
B 22.253	LILO	2–2	1950	
B 22.254	LILO	2–2	1950	
B 24.204	LVE	2	1905	Ex MBS.
B 24.284	LVE	2	1963	Ex ÖBB 7237.01. Post Van.

Standard Gauge Driving Trailers.

ES 22.230	LILO	2–2	1954
ES 22.231	LILO	2–2	1954
ES 22.232	LILO	2–2	1954
ES 22.233	LILO	2–2	1954
ES 22.234	LILO	2–2	1953
ES 22.235	LILO	2–2	1953
ES 22.236	LILO	2–2	1953

760 mm Gauge Railcars.

ET 23.101	GV	Bo	1912 110	30
ET 23.102	GV	Bo	1912 110	30
ET 23.103	VA	Bo	1921 110	30

ET 23.104	GV	Bo–Bo	1935	212	50	
ET 23.105	GV	Bo–Bo	1954	320	50	Ex Basel BDe 4/4 5.
ET 23.106	GV	Bo–Bo	1954	320	50	Ex Basel BDe 4/4 4.
ET 23.108	VA	Bo–Bo	1949	320	50	Ex AOMC BDe 4/4 111.
ET 23.109	GV	Bo–Bo	1951	320	50	Ex Basel BDe 4/4 8.
ET 23.110	GV	Bo–Bo	1951	320	50	Ex Basel BDe 4/4 9.
ET 26.101	VA	Bo	1912	90	30	
ET 26.106	VA	Bo–Bo	1936	212	50	
ET 26.107	VA	Bo–Bo	1936	212	50	
ET 26.109	VA	Bo–Bo	1949	212	50	Ex AOMC BDe 4/4 112.

760 mm Gauge Trailers.

B 20.220	VA	2	1907	Museum stock. Ex Gmünden 7.
B 20.222	VA	2	1907	Museum stock.
B 20.223	VA	2–2	1914	Ex VBW (Switzerland) 7.
B 20.224	VA	2–2	1914	Ex VBW (Switzerland) 7.
B 20.225	VA	2–2	1914	Ex VBW (Switzerland) 7.
B 20.226	VA	2–2	1914	Ex VBW (Switzerland) 7.
B 20.227	VA	2–2	1914	Ex VBW (Switzerland) 7.
B 20.228	VA	2–2	1914	Ex VBW (Switzerland) 7.
B 26.201	VA	2	1912	
B 26.250	VA	2	1912	

WIENER LOKALBAHN. (WLB)

A 30 km standard gauge line from Wien to Baden. Really more of a tramway but with freight traffic. Electrified at 650/88 V dc.

Depots: Wien Wolfganggasse. Inzersdorf. Leesdorf.
Timetable: 51a.

A 30 km standard gauge line from Wien to Baden. Really more of a tramway but with four diesel-hydraulic locos for freight traffic. Electrified at 650/800 V dc.

Number	Wheels	Built	kW	km/h	NAME or notes
V 80	C dh	1962	445	60	
V 81	B dh	1967	300	60	
V 82	C dh	1976	445	60	
V 83	C dh	1980	445	60	
07	Bo		160	50	Departmental.
11	Bo–2	1958	150	70	Ex Köln Tramway.
12	Bo–2	1958	150	70	Ex Köln Tramway.
13	Bo–2	1958	150	70	Ex Köln Tramway.
14	Bo–2	1958	150	70	Ex Köln Tramway.
15	Bo–2	1958	150	70	Ex Köln Tramway.
16	Bo–2	1958	150	70	Ex Köln Tramway.
17	Bo–2	1958	150	70	Ex Köln Tramway.
18	Bo–2	1958	150	70	Ex Köln Tramway.
19	Bo–2	1958	150	70	Ex Köln Tramway.
22	Bo–Bo	1927	264	70	
23	Bo–Bo	1927	264	70	
25	Bo–Bo	1927	264	70	
26	Bo–Bo	1927	264	70	
31	Bo–Bo	1928	264	70	
32	Bo–Bo	1927	264	70	Departmental.
41	2–2	1908			
43	2–2	1908			
46	2–2	1908			
47	2–2	1908			
48	2–2	1908			
49	2–2	1908			
54	2–2	1908			
101	B–2–2–B	1979	380	80	ERICH
102	B–2–2–B	1979	380	80	KARL
103	B–2–2–B	1979	380	80	THEO
104	B–2–2–B	1979	380	80	RUDI

105	B–2–2–B	1983	380	80	TONI
106	B–2–2–B	1983	380	80	LOISL
107	B–2–2–B	1983	380	80	HERI
108	B–2–2–B	1983	380	80	ERNST
109	B–2–2–B	1983	380	80	HANS
110	B–2–2–B	1983	380	80	HERTA
111	B–2–2–B	1987	380	80	INGE
112	B–2–2–B	1987	380	80	RENI
113	B–2–2–B	1987	380	80	VERA
117	2–2	1894			Retained as museum stock.
120	2–2	1899			Retained as museum stock.
200	1A–A1	1900	160		Retained as museum stock.
230	Bo–Bo	1928	264		Retained as museum stock.
256	2–2	1906			Retained as museum stock.
270	2–2	1950			Retained as museum stock.

Wiener Lokalbahn motor car 22 is seen with trailer 47 at Wien Wolfganggasse during June 1985.   *John Stein*

ZILLERTALBAHN (ZB)

A 31 km 760 mm gauge line from Jenbach to Mayrhofen.

Depots: Jenbach (main), Mayrhofen (subshed).

Number	Wheels	Built	kW	km/h	NAME or notes
2	0–6–2T	1900	160	35	ZILLERTAL
3	0–6–2T	1902	225	35	TIROL
5	0–6–2T	1930	250	40	GERLOS
6	0–4–0T	1916			
D 7	Bo–Bo de	1940	90	35	
D 8	D dh	1967	403	50	
D 9	D dh	1967	403	50	
D 10	BB dh	1970	440	50	Former JZ 740.007.
D 11	B dh	1960	104	20	
D 12	B dh	1958	104	20	
VT 1	3 car	1954	214		Ex Rotterdam Tramway.
VT 3	BB de	1985	228	70	Operates as 2/3/4 car set.
VT 4	BB de	1985	228	70	Operates as 2/3/4 car set.

▲Montafonerbahn railcar ET10.103 and trailer at Bludenz during February 1986 waiting to leave for Schruns. *John Stein*

▼E 27.001 operates on the Stern und Hafferl line between Bürmoos and Trimmelkam. It is owned by the colliery company SAKOG and is seen at Trimmelkam Colliery on 08/09/87. *Peter Fox*

MUSEUMS & MUSEUM LINES

Preservation in Austria has followed trends in other countries. There is a National collection which was recently enlarged when Austria celebrated 150 years of its railways. Additionally there are many preservation societies and museum lines. These normally operate at weekends only in the summer season. However, the visiting enthusiast will find other lines operating in the midweek period in the summer as ÖBB's two mountain rack lines use steam and some private railways have regular steam operations.

Also the many clubs, as well as ÖBB, operate excursions using vintage motive power. Station noticeboards and local railway magazines should always be consulted for details of coming events.

The lists of museums and museum lines is grouped into provinces and arranged in alphabetical order, and also includes steam operations on ÖBB and private commercial railways.

KÄRNTEN.

Kärnten Museumsbahnen (KMB).

An active society with three distinct operations.
  (1) Excursions on ÖBB lines in the area using their loco 93.1378.
  (2) Eurotram collection. Twelve metre gauge trams to be used over a restored line in Klagenfurt.
  (3) Gurktalbahn narrow gauge museum line (760 mm gauge). The society operates trains over a short remnant of a former ÖBB line at Pöckstein near Treibach Althofen.
16 steam, 6 diesel, 2 electric. The society also owns 20–30 600 mm gauge diesels which are in Graz for a planned museum there.

Lienz.

Verein der Eisenbahnfreunde, Lienz. This society owns 52.3816 which it uses from time to time over ÖBB lines in the area.

NIEDERÖSTERREICH.

Amstetten.

ÖBB locomotive depot. Österreichische Gesellschaft für Eisenbahn Geschichte (ÖGEG) restore locomotives here. Current activity is on Romanian Railways (CFR) 2–8–4 142.063. 78.618 is active.

Freiland.

Feld and Industriebahn Museum (FIM) 600 mm gauge. Located adjacent to ÖBB station. 2 steam, 22 diesel.

Gmünd.

ÖBB operates its own narrow gauge steam locos on excursion trains as well as on regular trains at weekends in the summer.Excursion trains also operate occasionally on the closed lines to Litschau and Heidenreichstein.

Payerbach–Reichenau–Hirschwang. 6.7 km.

760 mm. Electric 500 V dc. Österreichische Gesellschaft für Lokalbahnen (ÖGLB) operate steam, diesels, and electrics on this former industrial railway. The depot is at Hirschwang. 6 steam, 7 diesel, 3 electric, 2 trams.

52e Puchberg – Hochschneeberg. 9 km.

1000 mm. Not a museum line but one of the ÖBBs mountain rack lines. Regular steam operation over the line which starts at 577 metres above sea level and ends at 1795 metres above sea level.

Waidhofen an der Ybbs.

Club 598, Freunde der Ybbstalbahn. This group owns 598.02 which it uses from time to time over the ÖBB narrow gauge line (timetable 13a).

OBERÖSTERREICH.

Linz.

ÖBB Hauptwerkstatte. ÖGEG keeps some of its active locos here which are used on excursions over lines in the area.

St.Florian–Pichling Ort. 6 km.

900 mm. Museumsbahn St.Florian – Pichling Ort (MBF) is another ÖGEG operation located on the outskirts of Linz. Access by Postbus Line 2048 from Kleinmünchen or by tram from Linz. 9 trams, 3 diesel, 1 electric.

Grünberg–Steyr. 18 km.

760 mm. Steyrtalbahn, another ÖGEG operation over a closed ÖBB line. The depot is at Grünberg.
5 steam, 3 diesel.

SALZBURGLAND.

17c St.Wolfgang–Schafbergspitze. 6 km.

1000 mm. Regular steam operation over this ÖBB mountain line but beware – there are also two diesel railcars. The line rises from 540 metres to 1734 metres above sea level.

23. Zell am See–Krimml. 54 km.

760 mm. Occasional steam specials operate on this ÖBB line.

STEIERMARK.

Frojach.

Club 760, Freunde der Murtalbahn.A supporting group for the Steiermarkische Landesbahn line from Unzmarkt to Tamsweg. The group has its own museum at Frojach.
10 steam, 3 diesel.

Graz.

Steiermarkische Eisenbahnfreunde. StEF. A supporting organisation for the GKB. The society organises private excursions using the GKB steam locos over GKB and ÖBB lines in the area.

Graz.

Tramway Museum. Collection of 19 trams from cities in the former Austro-Hungarian territory.

Graz.

Feldbahn Museum. Not yet open to the public. Collection of KMB 600 mm gauge stock.
1 steam, 29 diesel, 2 electric.

Mariazell–Erlausee.

Museumstramway (MT). A purpose built line over which steam and electric trams are operated.
2 steam, 4 diesel, 18 trams.

63.Murau–Tamsweg.

Steiermarkische Landesbahn. (StLB). Regular steam operated trains are run over this section of line (usually tuesdays & wednesdays in the summer).

(63) Mauterndorf–Tamsweg. 12 km.

Taurachbahn GmbH. 760 mm. An offshoot of Club 760 which began operating over this closed part of the StLB line in summer 1988 using locos from its Frojach collection.

Stainz–Wohlsdorf. Stainzerbahn. 10.6 km.

760 mm. The local community supports tourism trains over this closed StLB line. 1 steam, 5 diesel.

52b. Weiz–Birkfeld. 24 km.

760 mm. StLB operates steam trains over their freight only line on WThSO in the summer.

TIROL.

Innsbruck. Zeughaus Museum.

This city museum has a railway section. 2 steam, 1 electric, 1 tram.

31. Jenbach–Mayrhofen. Zillertalbahn. 32 km.

760 mm. Regular steam trains in the summer season using the ZB steam locos. One loco is usually available for the public to drive!

31a. Jenbach–Achensee. Achenseebahn. 7 km.

1000 mm. Regular steam workings on this rack and adhesion line which rises from 532 metres above sea level to 931 metres above sea level with a summit at Eben of 970 metres.

VORARLBERG.

Bezau.

760 mm. A museum operation is being planned over the remaining part of the Bregenzerwaldbahn. 1 steam, 1 diesel.

42. Bludenz–Schruns. Montafonerbahn (MBS). 13 km.

1435 mm. This private line runs a Thursdays only steam train in the summer season using 178.84.

WIEN AREA.

Gross Schwechat.

Two societies are based here.

(1) Verband der Eisebahnfreunde (VEF) has a collection of standard gauge equipment which it operates from time to time over ÖBB lines around Wien. 4 diesels, 2 diesel railcars.

(2) Verein zur Förderung von Klein und Lokalbahnen. Another society specialising mostly in 600 mm gauge equipment for which there is a short demonstration line. 4 steam, 16 diesel, 3 electric.

Strasshof.

Eisenbahnmuseum "Das Heizhaus". This is located in the old ÖBB loco depot of Strasshof. Note that the nearest station to the museum is Silberwald and NOT Strasshof! A joint operation between "1. Österreichisches Strassenbahnen und Eisenbahn Klub" (1ÖSEK), ÖBB, and the Technical Museum. Most of the stock belongs to the national collection but there are some private items. The museum opens Sundays only. 24 steam, 1 diesel.

Wien Floridsdorf.

ÖBB Hauptwerkstatte and Zugförderungsleitung. Some operational museum stock is kept at these two locations for use on excursions around the Wien area. 1 steam, 4 electric, 1 EMU.

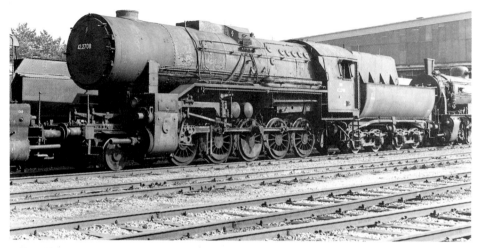

▲Das Heizhaus Museum, Strasshof, 20/09/87. 42.2708 is an example of the larger DRG 'Kriegslok' 2–10–0s.   *Colin Boocock*

▼580.03 is a 2–10–0 of the former Südbahn.   *Colin Boocock*

Wien Ostbahnhof.

ÖBB depot. Brenner und Brenner Dampflokomotiven Betriebsgesellschaft usually keep 3 or 4 locos here for use on excursion trains around the Wien area. Close by is the UIC Testing Plant of Wien Arsenal in Faradaygasse where ex-BR gas turbine loco 18000 is plinthed.

Wien Prater.

The famous Wien leisure park has a 381mm gauge railway system which uses 2 steam and 3 diesel.

Wien.

Österreichisches Eisenbahn Museum im Technischen Museum für Industrie und Gewerb, Mariahilferstrasse 212. Located close to the Westbahnhof there is a large railway section. Some locos are plinthed outside.
13 steam, 3 electric.

Wien Erdberg.

Wiener Strassenbahnmuseum, Erdbergstrasse 109. Wien has a fantastic tramway system with over 1800 trams in service! A wonderful selection of trams has been preserved by Wien Tramways, and supporting organisations such as VEF and Arge Oldtimer Tramway.

An attraction for British railway enthusiasts is ex BR Western Region gas-turbine No. 18000 which is plinthed at the Wien Arsenal testing station. It is known to the Austrians as 'Elisabetta'.   *Peter Fox*

▲The preserved Gölsdorf 2–6–4 310.23 poses at Gänserndorf on a 'Rail 150' steam special. The engine is a 4-cylinder compound and had a 43 year working life from 1911 to 1956.
Colin Boocock

▼4–6–2T 77.250 pilots 4–8–0 33.132 on an enthusiasts' special at Wiener Neustadt on 19/09/87.
Colin Boocock

PRESERVED LOCOMOTIVES & RAILCARS

STATUS CODES

A	Active (location may vary).		M	Museum or Museum line loco.
P	Plinthed ('Denkmal').		R	Under restoration (perhaps at another place).
K	Retained for special excursions.		S	Stored or for spares.

ÖBB STEAM LOCOMOTIVES:

Number	Wheels	Built	Status	Location
12.10	2–8–4	1936	M	TM Wien (Mariahilferstrasse 212)
15.13	2–6–2	1910	M	TM Wien (Mariahilferstrasse 212)
16.08	2–6–4	1911	MA	WN. Preserved as KKStB 310.23
30.33	2–6–2T	1897	MA	EM Strasshof
30.109	2–6–2T	1900	MR	Brenner & Brenner ÖBB HW St. Pölten
33.102	4–8–0	1923	M	TM Wien (Mariahilferstrasse 212)
"33.112"	4–8–0	1925	MA	Brenner & Brenner, WO
35.233	2–6–2	1916	M	EM Strasshof
38.4101	4–6–0	1912	M	EM Strasshof
42.2708	2–10–0	1946	M	EM Strasshof
42.2721	2–10–0	1947	MR	Pétange (Luxembourg)
50.685	2–10–0	1940	MA	H.E. Frankfurt/M (W. Germany)
50.1171	2–10–0	1942	K	GKB Graz
52.221	2–10–0	1943	M	Samstagern (Switzerland)
52.855	2–10–0	1944	MA	ÖBB HW Floridsdorf
52.1198	2–10–0	1943	MA	ÖGEG Bischofshofen
52.1227	2–10–0	1944	MR	Brenner & Brenner, HW St. Pölten
52.2436	2–10–0	1943	P	Japan
52.3314	2–10–0	1944	MR	Museums Eisenbahn Paderborn (W. Germany)
52.3316	2–10–0	1944	MA	ÖGEG Linz
52.3504	2–10–0	1943	MA	Luxembourg
52.3517	2–10–0	1943	MA	ÖGEG Linz
52.3816	2–10–0	1944	MA	Lienz
52.3879	2–10–0	1944	MA	Brenner & Brenner, LK
52.4552	2–10–0	1944	S	ÖBB HW Linz
52.5804	2–10–0	1943	M	Neuenmarkt Wirsberg (W. Germany)
52.7046	2–10–0	1943	P	Selzthal
52.7102	2–10–0	1943	P	Wien
52.7409	2–10–0	1943	P	Wurzburg 1 depot (W. Germany)
52.7593	2–10–0	1944	P	Strasshof (Bundesstrasse 205)
52.7594	2–10–0	1944	MA	EM Strasshof
52.7596	2–10–0	1944	MA	Singen (W. Germany)
52.7612	2–10–0	1944	MA	Brenner & Brenner, ÖBB HW St. Pölten
152.3109	2–10–0	1942	M	Sinsheim Museum (W. Germany)
152.4867	2–10–0	1942	MA	H.E. Frankfurt/M (W. Germany)
53.7101	0–6–0	1868	P	ÖBB Linz Hbf
153.7114	0–6–0	1869	M	Innsbruck
54.14	2–6–0	1899	M	TM Wien (Mariahilferstrasse 212)
55.5708	0–8–0	1887	M	TM Wien (Mariahilferstrasse 212)
56.3115	2–8–0	1913	K	GKB Graz
56.3255	2–8–0	1919	M	CSD Praha (Czechoslovakia)
156.3423	2–8–0	1920	M	TM Wien (Mariahilferstrasse 212)
57.223	0–10–0	1916	M	EM Strasshof
257.601	0–10–0	1921	M	EM Strasshof
257.605	0–10–0	1921	MS	EM Strasshof
58.774	2–10–0	1923	M	TM Wien (Mariahilferstrasse 212)
258.902	2–10–0	1912	M	EM Strasshof
69.02	2–2–2T	1898	M	EM Strasshof
770.86	2–4–0T	1913	P	Bhf Pochlarn

175.817	2–6–2T	1912	M	EM Strasshof
77.28	4–6–2T	1920	P	ÖBB Zfl LZ
77.66	4–6–2T	1913	M	EM Strasshof
77.244	4–6–2T	1927	MA	Brenner & Brenner WO
77.250	4–6–2T	1927	P	Schaan Vaduz (Lichtenstein)
78.606	4–6–4T	1931	P	Amstetten Eggersdorferstrasse
78.618	4–6–4T	1938	MA	ÖGEG Amstetten ÖBB depot
86.476	2–8–2T	1943	MR	ÖGEG Linz
088.01	0–4–0T	1906	M	EM Strasshof
789.837	0–6–0T	1921	M	BEM Nördlingen (West Germany)
989.01	0–6–0T	1944	M	Probstdorf
91.32	2–6–0T	1900	P	Bhf Mürzzuschlag
91.107	2–6–0T	1908	MA	Brenner & Brenner MZ
92.2220	0–8–0T	1898	P	Puchberg (near station)
92.2231	0–8–0T	1909	MA	Montafonerbahn Schruns
92.2234	0–8–0T	1910	S	EM Strasshof
92.2271	0–8–0T	1919	MA	Brenner & Brenner, WO
392.2510	0–8–0T	1927	M	EM Strasshof
392.2530	0–8–0T	1927	MA	ÖGEG Linz
93.1326	2–8–2T	1927	MR	ÖGEG WE
93.1332	2–8–2T	1927	MA	Regentalbahn (W. Germany)
93.1335	2–8–2T	1927	P	St. Andra (Zicksee)
93.1360	2–8–2T	1927	MA	Eurovapor - Fützen (W. Germany)
93.1364	2–8–2T	1927	P	Bhf Hainfeld
93.1378	2–8–2T	1927	MA	Klagenfurt ÖBB depot
93.1379	2–8–2T	1927	P	Bhf Schwarzach St. Veit
93.1394	2–8–2T	1927	MA	Eurovapor - Fützen (W. Germany)
93.1403	2–8–2T	1927	P	Leobersdorf Spielplatz
93.1410	2–8–2T	1928	MS	Exertalbahn, Rinteln (W. Germany)
93.1420	2–8–2T	1928	MA	Brenner & Brenner WO
93.1421	2–8–2T	1928	P	ÖBB HW Floridsdorf
93.1422	2–8–2T	1928	MA	Brenner & Brenner, WO
93.1434	2–8–2T	1928	P	ÖBB Depot Salzburg Gnigl
93.1455	2–8–2T	1931	MA	ÖGEG WE
694.503	0–10–0T	1913	P	Graz-Gosting
95.112	2–10–2T	1922	P	Bhf Payerbach
97.201	0–6–2T	1890	P	ÖBB HW Knittelfeld
97.203	0–6–2T	1890	P	ÖBB HW St. Pölten (entrance)
97.208	0–6–2T	1892	MA	EM Strasshof
97.210	0–6–2T	1893	M	Darmstadt Kranichstein (W. Germany)
97.217	0–6–2T	1908	P	Vordernberg Markt Hauptplatz
197.301	0–12–0T	1912	MA	EM Strasshof
297.401	2–12–2T	1941	P	Bhf Vordernberg
298.05	0–6–2T	1898	P	ÖBB HW Knittelfeld
298.06	0–6–2T	1898	S	ÖBB HW Knittelfeld
298.14	0–6–2T	1898	MR	Ochsenhausen (W. Germany)
298.24	0–6–2T	1902	P	Bregenz, Spielplatz am See
298.25	0–6–2T	1902	P	Eichgraben
298.51	0–6–2T	1898	MA	ÖGLB Hirschwang
298.52	0–6–2T	1898	MA	Grünburg Bhf
298.53	0–6–2T	1898	MA	Grünburg Bhf
298.54	0–6–2T	1898	P	Kirchberg
298.55	0–6–2T	1898	P	Bhf Mittersill
298.56	0–6–2T	1899	MS	HW KD for Club 760
298.102	0–6–2T	1888	M	KMB Treibach Althofen
298.104	0–6–2T	1890	MR	ÖGLB Hirschwang
298.106	0–6–2T	1914	MR	Grünburg Bhf
298.205	0–6–2T	1902	MR	ÖGLB Hirschwang
298.206	0–6–2T	1902	P	Langschlag Ortskern
398.01	0–6–2T	1905	A	Murau
498.03	0–6–2T	1929	P	Bhf Bezau
498.04	0–6–2T	1929	P	Bhf St. Veit a.d. Glan
498.06	0–6–2T	1930	MR	ÖGLB Grünberg
498.07	0–6–2T	1931	P	Obergrafendorf, ESV Sportplatz
498.08	0–6–2T	1931	M	KMB Treibach Althofen

598.01	0–6–4T	1896	MR	KMB Treibach Althofen
598.02	0–6–4T	1896	MA	Club 598, Waidhofen a.d. Ybbs (as Yv2)
598.03	0–6–4T	1896	MS	Club 598, Waidhofen a.d. Ybbs
698.01	0–4–0T	1941	P	Bhf Haag
798.01	0–6–0TT	1941	MA	Mockmühl (W. Germany)
898.01	0–6–0T	1941	MR	KMB, Treibach Althofen
199.02	0–8–2T	1926	M	KMB, Treibach Althofen
199.03	0–8–2T	1926	MS	Jugoslavia
299.01	0–8–4T	1907	S	ÖBB HW Knittelfeld
499.01	0–10–0T	1924	M	KMB, Treibach Althofen
699.01	0–8–0	1944	MA	Club 760, Frojach
699.02	0–8–0	1944	M	Club 760, Frojach
699.101	0–8–0T	1944	M	KMB, Treibach Althofen
699.103	0–8–0T	1944	MA	Grünburg Bhf
3071.07	2–4–2T	1935	M	EM Strasshof

ÖBB ELECTRIC LOCOMOTIVES:

Number	Wheels	Built	Status	Location
1018.05	1Do1	1939	MA	ÖBB Museum Lok LZ
1020.47	CoCo	1954	MA	ÖBB HW Floridsdorf
1060.01	1Co	1911	M	TM Wien (Mariahilferstrasse 212)
1161.012	D	1932	P	St. Veit a. d. Glan
1570.01	1ABoA1	1926	M	TM Wien etc.
1670.08	1ABoA1	1928	P	ÖBB Zfl IN (Westbhf)
1670.09	1ABoA1	1928	P	ÖBB Zfl IN (Westbhf)
1670.24	1ABoA1	1929	P	ÖBB Zfl BL
1670.25	1ABoA1	1929	MA	ÖBB Zfl Floridsdorf
1670.104	1ABoA1	1932	MA	ÖBB Zfl BL
1072.01	1B1	1913	MA	Privately owned. HW Floridsdorf
1072.05	1B1	1914	MS	Jedlersdorf
1073.03	1C1	1923	MS	ÖBB HW Linz
1280.14	E	1929	MS	ÖBB HW Linz
1985.02	Bo	1913	MA	Wien Gross Schwechat
1089.01	1CC1	1923	S	ÖBB HW Linz
1089.06	1CC1	1924	M	VHS Luzern (Switzerland)
1189.02	1CC1	1926	MA	ÖBB Museum Lok, HW Floridsdorf
1189.05	1CC1	1927	MA	ÖBB HW Floridsdorf
1189.09	1CC1	1927	P	ÖBB Wolfurt

ÖBB DIESEL LOCOMOTIVES:

Number	Wheels	Built	Status	Location
2020.01	BB dh	1959	P	ÖBB Zfl WO
2061.01	B dh	1940	MS	Wien Gross Schwechat
2190.01	Bo de	1934	MS	OGLB Hirschwang
2190.02	Bo de	1934	MS	OGLB Hirschwang
X111.04	B dm	1944	M	EM Strasshof

ÖBB ELECTRIC RAILCARS:

Number	Wheels	Built	Status	Location
4041.01	BoBo	1929	MA	ÖBB Zfl IN
4041.03	BoBo	1929	MA	ÖBB HW Floridsdorf
4041.05	BoBo	1929	MA	ÖBB Zfl IN

ÖBB DIESEL RAILCARS:

Number	Wheels	Built	Status	Location
5029.01	A–1 dm	1927	M	Gross Schwechat
5041.03	Bo–2 de	1933	M	ÖBB HW St. Pölten
5042.14	1AA1 de	1937	MA	ÖBB Zfl WN
5044.06	B–2 dh	1938	MA	ÖBB HW St. Pölten

1B1 1072.01 pilots "crocodile" 1189.05 pulling six 'Pressburgerbahn' coaches through Rennweg station (Wien) on 20/09/87.

Colin Boocock

OTHER RAILWAYS' STEAM LOCOMOTIVES:

Number	Rly	Wheels	Date	Status	Location
1.20	BBÖ	4–4–0	1883	M	TM Wien (Mariahilferstrasse 212)
494.62	BBÖ	0–6–0T	1887	P	Hohenau
827	BBÖ	4–4–0	1848	M	TM Wien (Mariahilferstrasse 212)
372	GKB	4–4–0	1891	MA	EM Strasshof
406	GKB	4–4–0	1896	MS	Grosuplje, Jugoslavia
415	GKB	4–4–0	1897	MA	Brenner & Brenner, NS
674	GKB	0–6–0	1860	M	TM Budapest (Hungary)
680	GKB	0–6–0	1860	MS	MVT Berlin
1851	GKB	0–6–0T	1898	MS	EM Strasshof
17	GySEV	0–6–0	1885	MA	Sopron (Hungary)
121	GySEV	2–6–2T	1914	P	Neufeld/Leitha
122	GySEV	2–6–2T	1916	P	Bad Neusiedl
123	GySEV	2–6–2T	1925	S	Fertöboz (Hungary)
324.1518	GySEV	2–6–2	1910	P	Sopron (Hungary)
424.140	GySEV	4–8–0	1941	P	Fertöboz (Hungary)
520.030	GySEV	2–10–0	1943	P	Fertöboz (Hungary)
37	KFN	0–4–2	1841	M	TM Wien (Mariahilferstrasse 212)
94 LICAON	KFN	2–4–0ST	1851	MA	WN
97.73	KKStB	0–6–0T	1894	P	Linz Hbf
180.1	KKStB	0–10–0	1900	M	TM Wien (Mariahilferstrasse 212)
229.222	KKStB	2–6–2T	1918	M	EM Strasshof
S 4	SKGLB	0–6–2T	1890	P	Pfandl, Bad Ischl
S 5	SKGLB	0–6–2T	1890	R	ÖBB HW Knittelfeld
S 9	SKGLB	0–6–2T	1893	P	Mondsee
Kh 111	StLB	0–10–0T	1930	M	Club 760, Frojach
S 7	StLB	0–6–2T	1893	M	Club 760, Frojach
S 11	StLB	0–6–2T	1894	MA	Stainz
U 8	StLB	0–6–2T	1894	P	Birkfield
U 9	StLB	0–6–2T	1894	P	St. Pölten Hbf (as "298.09")
U 11	StLB	0–6–2T	1894	M	Club 760, Frojach
Z 6	StLB	0–6–0T	1893	M	Club 760, Frojach
852	SB	0–6–0	1869	M	Zeughaus Museum, Innsbruck
1665	SB	0–6–0	1895	M	EM Strasshof
290c	Sulm	0–6–0T	1907	S	Bleiburg
1	ZB	0–6–2T	1900	M	Zeughaus Museum, Innsbruck

OTHER RAILWAYS' DIESEL & ELECTRIC:

Number	Rly	Wheel Arr.	Date	Status	Location
RT 2	StLB	B dm	1941	A	Club 760, Frojach
VL 01	StLB	D dh	1942	A	Club 760, Frojach
ET 23.101	St&H	Bo e	1912	R	Eurotram, Klagenfurt
ET 26.101	St&H	Bo e	1912	R	Eurotram, Klagenfurt
ABmot 12	GySEV	A–1 dm	1926	S	Fertöboz (Hungary)

CODES

DEPOT CODES

The ÖBB is divided into four divisions ('Direktionen'). In each division are several 'Zugförderungsleitungen' (Zf). These are depots with full maintenance facilities which are capable of carrying out heavy repairs. Other depots ('Zugförderungsstellen' – Zfs) only carry out lighter maintenance. These are as follows:

P5 Code	ÖBB Code	Depot	P5 Code	ÖBB Code	Depot
AM	Ams	Zfl Amstetten	PB	Pc	Zfs Puchberg
AT	At	Zfs Attnang-Puchheim	SP	Pb	Zfl St. Pölten
BO	Bo	Zfs Bischofshofen	SW	Zd	Zfs St. Wolfgang
BL	Bl	Zfl Bludenz	SL	Sl	Zfs Selzthal
FD	F	Zfl Floridsdorf (Wien)	SB	Sb	Zfl Salzburg
GM	Gm	Zfs Gmünd	VH	Vt	Zfl Villach
GZ	Gz	Zfl Graz	WE	We	Zfl Wels
IN	In	Zfl Innsbrück West	WF	Wf	Zfl Wien FJB
KD	Kd	Zfl Knittelfeld	WH	Wh	Zfs Waidhofen a.d. Ybbs
KR	Bk	Zfs Krems	WL	W	Zfs Wörgl
LE	Lie	Zfs Lienz	WN	Nw	Zfl Wien Nord
LK	Le	Zfs Landeck	WO	Of	Zfl Wien Ost
LZ	Lz	Zfl Linz	WS	Wb	Zfl Wien Sud
MZ	Mz	Zfs Mürzzuschlag	WW	Ws	Zfl Wien West
NS	Nb	Zfl Wiener Neustadt	ZS	Z	Zfs Zell am See

LIVERY CODES

B   Railbus livery (blue/white).
C   New diesel railcar livery (cream/blue/red).
D   Old diesel railcar livery (blue/cream).
E   Standard EMU livery (cream/blue).
G   Green.
M   Mariazellerbahn loco. livery (red/cream).
N   New cream/orange loco livery.
O   Other non-standard livery - refer to text.
R   New narrow gauge diesel railcar livery (cream/red).
S   S-bahn livery (cream/blue).
T   Transalpin livery (cream/blue with red around headlights).

ABBREVIATIONS USED

The following additional abbreviations are used in the 'Preserved locomotives & Multiple Units' and 'Other Austrian Railways' sections:

CFR   Caile Ferate Romäne (Rumanian State Railways).
CSD   Československé Státni Drahy (Czechoslavakian State Railways).
DB   Deutsche Bundesbahn (German Federal Railways).
JZ   Jugoslovenske Železnice (Yugoslavian State Railways).
MÁV   Magyar Államvasutak (Hungarian State Railways).
SOB   Sudostbahn.
SS   Südliche Staatsbahn.
SKGLB   Salzkammergut Lokalbahn.
EM   Eisenbahn Museum.
HE   Historische Eisenbahn.
ÖGEG   Österreichische Gesellschaft für Eisenbahn Geschichte.
ÖGLB   Österreichische Gesellschaft für Lokalbahnen.
TM   Technical Museum.

Outside back cover Photograph: The 14.00 Gmünd–Gross Gerungs (Waldviertelbahn) on 12/09/87 hauled by 'Engerth' 399.05 takes water at Bruderndorf. Certain well-oiled members of an 'oompah' band can be seen sitting on the water-crane supply pipe.   *Peter Fox*